The Root of Roots

Melville and Frances Herskovits setting off upriver, 9 July 1929

The Root of Roots:
Or, How Afro-American Anthropology Got Its Start

Richard Price & Sally Price

PRICKLY PARADIGM PRESS
CHICAGO

© 2003 Richard Price and Sally Price
All rights reserved.

Prickly Paradigm Press, LLC
5629 South University Avenue
Chicago, Il 60637

www.prickly-paradigm.com

ISBN: 0-9728196-2-2
LCCN: 2003111001

Printed in the United States of America on acid-free
paper.

Complete notes for this pamphlet, including page references to the Herskovitses' diaries, as well as acknowledg-
ments and bibliography, can be found on the web at:
www.prickly-paradigm.com/catalog.html

Quotations from the diaries and other field materials of
Melville and Frances Herskovits are reproduced courtesy of
the Literary Representative for the Works of Melville J. and
Frances S. Herskovits, Schomburg Center for Research in
Black Culture, The New York Public Library, Astor, Lenox
and Tilden Foundations.

Photos courtesy of: Eliot Elisofon Photographic Archives,
National Museum of African Art, Smithsonian Institution
(frontispiece, pp. 6, 65, 73); Melville J. and Frances S.
Herskovits Photograph Collection, Photographs and Prints
Division, Schomburg Center for Research in Black Culture,
The New York Public Library, Astor, Lenox and Tilden
Foundations (pp. 19 and 31); National Anthropological
Archives, Smithsonian Institution (p. 12); NewYork Weill
Cornell Medical Center Archives (p. 35); Unitätsarchiv in
Herrnhut, Germany (Nr. 5185) (p. 27); Melville J. and
Frances S. Herskovits, *Rebel Destiny* (1934), facing p. 332 (p.
45); Silvia W. de Groot, *Djuka Society and Social Change*
(1969), facing p. 56 (p. 47).

2 August 1929, Asindoopo, Suriname: "A worse day,—and an anxious one.... We're alone in the interior and... what will happen no one can say, but we held a council of war and decided to act fast. We called [the chief] in after supper and told him... we'd like to leave.... The larger number of men who are about, and the general atmosphere, are anything but reassuring.... Neither of us to sleep very much.... Because if they're afraid of what we learned, anything is possible; we're watching our food & water."

(Melville J. Herskovits field diary)

These days, when a way of life is being killed off, or eroding so fast that no one can quite grasp what's happening, the state often raises a monument to celebrate it. In fact, the museumification of a culture—its admittance into the national patrimony—is frequently the clearest sign of its demise.

The same might be said of academic disciplines. The sudden rise of interest in the history of anthropology—countless books and articles analyzing and celebrating everyone from (in last year's crop) Papa Franz Boas and his early years in Germany to Sir Edmund Leach, who left us just over a decade ago—

seems part of a larger process of pastification. As the people anthropologists once studied die out (or become more "just like us"), cultural and literary studies and cognate approaches have been queuing up to handle their academic appropriation. Anthropology itself may well be in the process of becoming a relic.

Nonetheless the two of us, like a couple of thousand other throw-backs, continue to practice anthropology, going to "the field," writing books, and increasingly engaging in human rights and other activist work in collaboration with the people we have long studied, in our case the Saramaka Maroons of Suriname, descendants of rebel slaves who escaped to the South American rain forest in the seventeenth and early eighteenth centuries and built a vibrant African-American culture and society that still flourishes—despite mounting threats from multinational logging and mining companies.

We first encountered Saramakas in 1966 (after six summers of fieldwork in other parts of the world), and we've spent much of our lives learning and writing about their culture. Melville and Frances Herskovits, who pioneered the field of Afro-American anthropology, engaged Saramakas more briefly, over the course of two summer visits in 1928 and 1929. It was their first foreign fieldwork.

And yet, what the Herskovitses took away from those two Saramaka summers played a pivotal role in the development of both Afro-American Studies and African Studies in the North American academy and continues to shape current debates about the African Diaspora. No one—whether historian, anthropologist, sociologist, or literary critic—can ignore the fiery debates kindled by the Herskovitses' visits to 1920s Saramaka. As one critic recently put it, the Saramaka have by now become "a sort of anthropological metonym...providing the exemplary arena in which to argue out certain anthropological claims about a discursive domain called Afro-America."

So it was with considerable excitement that we learned last year (through the kindness of a colleague, Kevin Yelvington) that the Herskovitses' daughter had made her parents' handwritten field diaries from those summers available for consultation at the Schomburg Center for Research on Black Culture in New York.

Unpacking the moment of high anxiety that abruptly terminated the Herskovitses' stay in the village of the Saramaka paramount chief will help shed light on the ways in which early twentieth-century ideas about race, gender, science, authenticity, and the nature of culture contributed to the initial conception of the field we now call Afro-American Studies. In following their experience, as recorded in the field diaries, we see how U.S. racism—as well as the 1920s New York liberals' romance with things black—shaped the discourse. We see how the strength of ideas about science and method often trumped the actual findings, and how the research itself was caught up in a web of colonial practices. We witness the search for the real McCoy, for cultural artifacts and knowledge that are pure and ancient. To the beat of the drums, we witness the discovery of Africa in the Americas. And along the way, we learn that Frances Shapiro Herskovits, though constrained by the gender rules of the day, played a particularly decisive role, serving as midwife to the somewhat painful birth of a discipline.

The 1928 and 1929 Field Trips

The Saramaka fieldwork was pivotal in Melville Herskovits' career, exercising—in the words of his widow—"a profound influence on his thinking."

> In the Guiana bush...he saw, as he often told his students, nearly all of western sub-Saharan Africa represented, from what is now Mali to Loango and into the Congo—and the Loango chief who came to our base camp [in Saramaka] invoked both the Great God of the Akan of the Gold Coast, *Nyankompon*, and the Bantu *Zambi*.

During that research, and on the voyages to and from Suriname, he developed a comparative vision of Afro-American studies (and of the Caribbean as "a social laboratory") that would fuel his own prodigious work, and that of countless students, for decades to come. The seeds of his interest in exploring the African provenience of New World Negroes, in establishing an historical-ethnographic baseline in Africa for the study of New World developments, and in analyzing processes of cultural change (such as "acculturation," "reinterpretation," and "syncretism") were all sown during this early fieldwork.

On 22 June 1928, Melville and Frances Herskovits (hereafter MJH or "Herskovits" and FSH or "Fann") set out from New York bound for Suriname aboard the steamship Cottica. They are accompanied by Morton C. Kahn, a physician who has conducted an epidemiological study among the Saramaka "Bush Negroes" (as Maroons were then called) and will accompany MJH into the interior. Thirty-three years old, five years beyond his Ph.D. under Boas at Columbia, and a year into his assistant professorship of anthropology at Northwestern, MJH is about to launch his first experience as a fieldworker outside the USA. Following the advice of Kahn and others familiar with the rigors of travel in the rain forest, he has made arrangements for his wife of four years to remain in Paramaribo, the capital city, while he journeys upriver to make preliminary contact with Saramakas. MJH's diaries and field notes from that summer and the next, when the couple returned for further work, allow us to follow his experience day by day. (To our regret, FSH's diaries and field notes from Saramaka are relatively brief.)

Arriving in Suriname on July 10, the Herskovitses quickly move into their Paramaribo hotel and are introduced to their cook—"Duffy by name, and black as the well-known ace of spades. He'll run errands for us here and cook and interpret up-river, and be our boy when we return, for $1 a day." (He's been hired for them by Kahn, who had volunteered to "have our outfit all ready upon arrival [so] we will not lose the week in Paramaribo which would be necessary to gather same together.") Their main preoccupations are the various health problems MJH has suffered during the voyage, which now have

FSH with the person we believe to be Duffy (Paramaribo, 1928)

him in bed under a doctor's care, and the need to find an informant for FSH's ethnographic work in the city.

By the 13th, FSH has arranged to begin paid interviews with Duffy's wife, Jacoba Abensitt ("a literate young woman"), and on the 17th MJH reports that she's "a find—intensely superstitious, and yet willing to talk." The head of the colony's forestry service, E. W. Rogalli, hired by Kahn as MJH's guide for the summer, has been released for the purpose by the Colonial Secretary, and he begins working closely with MJH (doing the shopping in preparation for the trip to Saramaka, bringing in artifacts to buy, and together with his German wife hosting the Herskovitses for tea at what MJH describes as a comfortable private house with a garden). It is Rogalli who brings Herskovits, still bed-ridden, the Colonial Library's first edition of John Gabriel Stedman's eighteenth-century *Narrative, of a five years' expedition, against the Revolted Negroes of Surinam*. And from his bed, MJH begins an eleven-day series of formal interviews with W. F. van Lier, a Surinamer of Dutch-Jewish ancestry who is an authority on the Aucaner (Ndyuka) Bush Negroes of eastern Suriname, who already has seven published articles to his name, and who will go on to write another two dozen; in intensive sessions lasting many hours a day, they run systematically through Bush Negro kinship, marriage, village organization, law, religion, and beliefs—all in English, which van Lier speaks well. Van Lier, writes Herskovits, is a mine of information...and has...a more scientific attitude toward the data than anyone I've met so far.... We will have more talks, and I should get material from him of a type impossible to get in a short stay in the field and which should constitute valid information and an excellent set of leads for future work. For obviously, with only two weeks in the bush, my work will almost have to lie in the realm of material culture.... He certainly gives me a lot...It's all clean notes.... He has a real ethnological interest, even if it is an untrained one, and if the stuff I get in all its detail isn't correct he sure is the prize boy to see things wrong.

Van Lier also brings Herskovits four "Djukas," who visit briefly and provide kin terms and words in the ritual language of Kromanti. Van Lier, who has just left his job as government postholder among the Ndyuka, requests payment for his services as informant (which MJH reluctantly gives) and asks to accompany Herskovits upriver as guide, but other arrangements have been made by Kahn and, in any case, MJH feels too competitive to want him along. (By this time, MJH has also received close coaching on Bush Negro ethnography from a Dutch ethnographer, L. C. van Panhuys, who had been providing page after page of English-language summaries of relevant journal articles from Dutch and other European publications, including his own many contributions; this epistolary relationship continues for years.)

By July 24, MJH has recovered enough to undertake travel, and sets off by train and then river dugout for the camp of Alexander M. W. Wolff, manager of the Suriname Balata Company warehouse near the Christian Saramaka village of Gansee, which becomes his base camp.

> About two hours and a half after the start [of the canoe ride], we came to the landing, with Kahn looking well but a bit tired, and Duffy and Bundel there too with supper ready.... We've a nice hut right near the river and everything's very pleasant and snug.... [Kahn] will leave [upriver on a brief collecting trip] day after tomorrow (Thursday), and I'll spend until Monday at least here, working here with Schmidt, the Moravian Djuka convert-school-master and at Lombé and Gandje across the river.... By [evening] our hammocks and nets were slung, and after a bath in the moonlight but <u>not</u> in the river (electric eels and pirana preventing) I tried the hammock.... Rogali showed me how to arrange myself diagonally so that I'd lie straight.

In short, Kahn has already set up the team that will constitute Herskovits' entourage that summer. Wolff is their joint host in the base camp, as well as a frequent interpreter and informant, and the person who sets up all of MJH's dealings with Saramakas. Duffy (Rudolf Ubergen), brought from the city, is the cook but doubles as informant/interpreter. MJH's inseparable guide is Rogalli, a self-described "white bush negroe"—MJH comments that he "reads a great deal, is something of a socialist,...a man with wide interests. I like the way he loves his bush." Edwin Bundel, Rogalli's Afro-Surinamese assistant from Paramaribo (sometimes referred to by MJH as his "boy") becomes another of MJH's frequent inter-preter/informants—"He's a good man—has been years in the bush and knows a great deal about plant lore." R. M. Schmidt, headmaster of the Moravian school at Gansee, becomes Herskovits' main Saramaka-born informant. All these men are literate, speak decent English, and are paid for their services.

During the winter of 1928-29, preparing for the second and final expedition to Suriname, MJH sends out letters in hopes of hiring Rogalli and Bundel again, but they have already agreed to accompany Kahn up the Marowyne River in eastern Suriname. So Marcus J. Schloss, a professional guide whom the Herskovitses met at the home of James Lawton (the American consul in the colony), takes Rogalli's place, and Frederik Bekker (a city Creole normally employed by Wolff and the "main infor-mant" for the Herskovitses' Paramaribo folklore texts) is taken on as cook. Wolff is also hired as part of the second summer's team for the upriver trip to the village of the Saramaka *granman* (paramount chief). And Jacoba is hired as maid but is also used as informant. (She later takes over as expedition cook when Fred becomes ill.)

MJH's 1928 trip to Saramaka territory (during which FSH stayed in Paramaribo) lasts seventeen days:

July 24-30 are spent in Wolff's camp, with visits to two neighboring villages (missionized by the Moravians and Roman Catholics, respectively) and to a garden camp. On these visits, MJH is always accompanied by Kahn, Rogalli, Bundel, and/or Schmidt. He's also conducting interviews with these men (as well as, on one day, with a literate Saramaka from the Christian village of Futunakaba), on such subjects as dance, social organization, and religion. And he is recording scenes with his 16-millimeter movie camera and beginning to collect artifacts.

July 31-August 2 are devoted to river travel upstream, with stops in three or four villages along the way to collect artifacts.

August 3-4 is the return downstream to Wolff's camp, with two or three stops along the way. MJH travels in style. "Toward the stern [of the canoe] a 'tent' of broad palm leaves has been built, and in it windows which allow me to look out have been cut. Directly behind me the steersman sits and in front of me, under the shade, is Rogalli's chair...and near the bow, on a cross-seat, Bundel sits. The bow paddler is in front, at the very fore of the boat.... At about half-past one lunch was ready.... It doesn't take long to get settled, certainly your cannister and some boxes of food, Rogalli's folding table and the chairs, and there you are!"

August 5-8 is spent in Wolff's camp, with MJH's diary ending on August 5: "It was a quiet day."

August 9: MJH returns to Paramaribo, where Frances has been working on their ethnography of Creoles (Afro-Surinamers).

Frames from MJH's 1928 movies—
Rogalli in Gansee, Jacoba and Frances in Paramaribo

The Herskovitses leave for New York, apparently aboard the Nickerie on August 17, and reach New York in mid-September, just in time for the opening of the International Congress of Americanists, where MJH presents his first paper on the Saramakas.

The 1929 trip to Saramaka territory, on which FSH accompanied him, was both longer and more eventful.

July 9: MJH and FSH, accompanied by their guide Schloss, their cook Fred, their maid Jacoba, and MJH's main informant Schmidt (whom MJH had summoned to Paramaribo for interviews), travel by train and canoe to Wolff's balata camp, where Wolff is waiting for them.

July 10-17: they're based at Wolff's camp, with forays to two neighboring villages. They conduct interviews with Schmidt, Schloss, and a Saramaka named Lalani, see funeral rites, including dancing, singing, drumming, and coffin divination, and make recordings of songs on their wax-cylinder "reproducer." A young Saramaka, Amonika/Tutú, who is hired as one of their canoemen by Wolff, befriends them.

July 18-26: travel upriver, going ashore (often for just a few minutes) at ten villages along the way, and arriving at the Saramaka chief's village on the afternoon of the 26th.

July 27: first full day of an intended two-week stay in the chief's village.

August 4: premature departure from the chief's village, on the pretext that their cook is ill.

August 5-7: return trip downstream to Wolff's camp.

August 8-14: at Wolff's camp, interviewing and collecting artifacts.

August 15: return to Kabelstation, the end of the train line from Paramaribo.

August 16-19: in and around the Sara Creek Ndyuka village of Koffiekamp, just downstream from Kabel, collecting artifacts and interviewing the local missionary.

The notes do not record the date of the Herskovitses' return to Paramaribo, but they are collecting Creole folklore texts there on August 23. They spend the end of August gathering texts and doing interviews for a book, *Suriname Folk-lore* (published in 1936). On September 5, they board the ship for New York, visiting several islands along the way, as MJH develops his ideas about how different New World peoples can be placed along a continuum from "most to least African": "On our way home through the eastern chain of the West Indian islands we were able, during the long calls which our boat made at various ports, to connect the Surinam Negroes very definitely with those of these islands. This gives us the connecting link through Porto Rico and the Bahamas to the negroes of the United States." Or, FSH writing years later: "My husband began outlining [these ideas] on board a cargo boat that was taking us...to the United States in the late summer of 1929.... In Barbados, Antigua, St. Lucia,

St. Kitts, and Dominica, he played the African game *wari* (which he had learned in Suriname) with the men on the docks, and talked to them about his stay among the Bush Negroes.... He was already well on his way into his ethnohistorical researches." MJH had already positioned the Saramakas he'd discovered in the deep interior of Suriname at the "African" end of a continuum whose other pole lay far away in the urban United States.

Looking for Africa

"A Dutchman on board from Paramaribo...says that the town- and Bush Negroes speak differently— '50% more African in the Bush taki.' Always there's the attempt to find the African—I'm not sorry to have had Elsie's skepticism. It may prevent my seeing too much African!"

MJH's allusion to the temptation to see "too much African" bespeaks a tension he lived with throughout the summers in Suriname—knowing in the abstract that trans-Atlantic connections should be historically grounded, but eager to discover as many specific traces of Africa as he could. In 1927, Kahn had described his own recent expedition to Herskovits—"I went 150 miles into the bush negro country.... I found these people to smack very noticeably of Africa, i.e., insofar as my limited information of the Dark Continent would allow"—and sent him "roto-gravure images" of Bush Negroes with the query, "Do they look African to you?" MJH replied, "They certainly look like West Africans and, as far as I can see, much of their culture is directly from the place of their origin." Herskovits considered Gerhard Lindblom's *Afrikanische Relikte...in der Kultur der Busch-Neger Surinams* "one of the most valuable things on the Bush Negroes" and prepared for his Saramaka fieldwork by "working with a Kru informant from West Africa so that I have a certain familiarity with the West African languages which will help me."

By 1928, Herskovits had built up a considerable store of knowledge about Africa, having written his Ph.D. dissertation, based on library sources, on "The Cattle Complex in East Africa," lectured at Columbia and Howard on African cultures, and prepared himself for a large comparative research project, which would have involved fieldwork in West Africa as well as various New World sites (but which was not in the end funded). He had already moved considerably away from his 1925 assimilationist position regarding the American Negro in which, in his contribution to Alain Locke's *The New Negro*, he asserted that there was "not a trace" of African culture in Harlem, toward an interest in the possibility that there might be African "remnants," for example in the motor behavior of black Americans. (In 1927, he remarked of Zora Neale Hurston, who was then serving as his research assistant, that her "manner of speech, her expressions,—in short, her motor behavior" could have been "handed down thru imitation and example from the original African slaves who were brought here.") Unlike the great bulk of Boas' students, who were carving out their careers in American Indian studies (a field that held a near monopoly over the articles published in the *American Anthropologist* and the *American Journal of Folklore*), Herskovits was at this time busy claiming Africa as his own bailiwick—a somewhat risky career move that at once isolated and energized him.

From New York to Paris, the romance of the "jungle" and the "negro" was very much in the air. On weekend evenings, fashionable New Yorkers were venturing into what they called "the black belt," north of 125th Street, and John Vandercook's *Tom-Tom*, a 1926 travelogue about Saramakas that the Herskovitses carried with them to Suriname in 1928, was preaching that "The civilized negro must lose his contempt for his 'heathen' brethren in Africa and in the jungles of...Suriname. He must learn that the fathers of the race had and still possess blessed secrets, wonderful lores, and great philosophies, that rank the jungle negro's civilization as the equal, and in many respects the superior, of any way of life that is to be found anywhere in the world." (It also reported as fact that "So vain are the [Saramakas] of their magnificent physiques that all young men who do not attain a stature of at least six feet are driven out to die.")

Throughout his stays in Saramaka country, MJH was "seeing Africa." (MJH had written before leaving for Suriname that "my primary interest is the obtaining of data which may assist in the solution of the problem of the provenience of the Negroes who are found in the Caribbean region and the United States." And FSH, thinking back on the Saramaka fieldwork many years later, stressed that "this was still the period in his research when the emphasis was on African carry-overs—'pure' Africanisms—for he was seeking firm leads that would point to regional and tribal origins of the African-derived populations of the New World.") The initial interview with W. F. van Lier dealt with "the organization of the courts, which looks very African to me," and the next day "I got relationship terms and some of the Kromanti talk, which sounds to me to be very African." Soon after, he described an "Indian axe-head which...Djukas... had found in the ground, and insisted was a bolt thrown from the sky by the Gods. Another Africanism, I'm sure—they appear at all sort of unex-pected places."

Having settled in his base camp, Herskovits is taken for his first look at a Saramaka village. "Just beyond was what I imagine was an important fetish [that]...looked very African altho I only got a glance at it.... The village as a whole, certainly looks like pictures from Africa—Congo and West." Several days later, he visits the village once more: "It is African. The houses and the fetishes, the naked children and the cicatrised grown-ups, all fit in." And by the end of his first week at the base camp, he concluded that, "The African remnant paper commends itself more and more to me, and I should have a mass of material for it before I am through."

During the rest of that summer and the next, MJH made frequent remarks about Africa in his diaries: a mankala (*wari*) game board is "the most indisputably African thing I've seen since I've been here.... [The Granman's son-in-law] was a real gentleman—So the African nobility holds here, too.... Much African hallooing from the women.... The iron pots on sticks with white clay heavily plastered on them are reminiscent of Ashanti."

But Herskovits wasn't just "seeing" Africa. He was inducing it and insisting on it repeatedly, through

MJH with Saramaka artifacts (Northwestern University, 1928)

speech and through pictures, instructing Saramakas about the origins of their practices from his first weeks there: "Lalani...said that when they returned from digging the corpse would be asked to tell who had killed him (in the African fashion, as I explained to him)." And during the second summer, the Herskovitses also came equipped with a "simple projector, actually a flashlight with a lens attached, through which a roll of film passed to flash images, one by one, on a screen."

> The illustrations we had photographed were from volumes on the people of the West Coast of Africa.... pictures of cicatrizations, of hairdressing and teeth filing, of rafts floating on African lakes, of pottery making and cloth weaving, of laying fires and the doing of other household tasks, of carvings, and, finally, of one or two priests and priestesses in states of possession.

They frequently showed these, and other African images from books they had brought along (R. S. Rattray's *Religion and Art in Ashanti* is the most frequently mentioned), and explained them to Saramakas, recording their reactions in the diaries.

> Fann...showed them pictures of Ashanti stools, and said they recognized all.... I am gradually showing more pictures of Africa, which astound [Granman Djankuso] and all his Captains assembled.... I showed African pictures to the two Kapteins of Dahomey, and I thought they'd fall off their stools. The stuff is certainly making an impression.... In

the evening I showed the African pictures with the projector; the old fellow and the rest of the village were there.

As they depict such scenes in *Rebel Destiny: Among the Bush Negroes of Dutch Guiana* (1934), ideas about Africa, power, and secrecy are often conjoined.

In the other corner, Chief And'u, the bassia, and about half a dozen men were talking of the great book about their ancestors which the white man had.

..."People say it has in it pictures of the Apuku gods, small as we ourselves know them, and a picture of the evil Apuku who appear as fire in the distance—Mati, white men have gone into the Kromanti houses in the country of our ancestors and have made pictures!"

"It is impossible!"

"I want to see!"

The old man said, "I will not look. Books are not for us, mati."... He would have nothing of pictures that figured what should never have been allowed to be photographed.

It seemed prudent to give the conversation a new turn.

Examples abound of the Herskovitses "Africanizing" Saramakas in their publications. They attribute to their canoemen the exclamation *"mfundu,"* which they explain means "deep." In fact, the Saramaccan word for "deep," today as in the eighteenth-century, is *fundu*, from Portuguese *fundo*, and the "African" phoneme "mf" does not exist in

Saramaccan. Or, again, the glossary that closes *Rebel Destiny*, written after the Herskovitses had done field-work in Dahomey and visited Ashanti, stretches even harder for a connection: "*Mamadam*, the great falls of the Saramacca.... It is difficult to determine the exact African parallel for this. An important sacred lake in Dahomey is called *Nohwe*—'house of our mother.' The word *dam* in Ashanti means 'room' and *mama* has our own connotation. In Ashanti a tributary of the sacred *Tano* river is called *Aberewa* meaning 'old woman.'" We would simply note that in standard Saramaccan, *mama* means "mother" and *dam* or *dan* "rapids" or "falls." *Mamadan* might appropriately be glossed, without recourse to convoluted African etymologies, as "Mother [of All] Rapids." And in *Rebel Destiny*, the Herskovitses quote a proverb containing the Saramaccan word *bulí* (meaning "to stir up"), which was recorded in that form as early as 1778 by a Moravian missionary and derives from the Portuguese *bulir* ("to stir"). But in their transcription, the word takes on an "African" phonology, "*gbuli*," and else-where MJH expressed considerable "excitement" when he "found a couple more examples of the 'gb' sound" in an interview with Schmidt. (The phoneme "gb" does indeed occur in Saramaccan—e.g., in *gbamba*, meaning "meat or fish"—but it does not occur in *bulí*.)

It is to the Herskovitses' credit that they some-times allowed their enthusiasm about "seeing Africa" to be reined in by the sort of scientific skepticism expressed by their patron, anthropologist/folklorist/philanthropist Elsie Clews Parsons. In a 1930 article on "Bush Negro Art" they conclude that "These people...have evolved an art form that, in many respects, may be considered to be a new one, for the Africanists who have seen the specimens...could not identify them with the art products of any definite area," and the "African remnants" paper that MJH was planning in 1928 turned into the much more nuanced 1930 *American Anthropologist* article in which he suggests for the first time the idea of "a scale for the intensity of Africanisms." The Herskovitses did not often indulge in the sensationalist titles of some of their contemporaries—Vandercook's "We Find an African Tribe in the South American Jungle," van Panhuys' "African Customs and Beliefs Preserved for Two Centuries in the Interior of Dutch Guiana," or Kahn's "Africa's Lost Tribes in South America: An On-the-Spot Account of Blood-Chilling African Rites of 200 Years Ago Preserved Intact in the Jungles of South America by a Tribe of Runaway Slaves." But they did state baldly in that same 1930 article on "Bush Negro Art": "The Bush-Negroes of Dutch Guiana...having remained faithful to their African traditions, present the unique phenomenon of an autonomous civilization of one continent—Africa—transplanted to another—South America," and MJH's first brief publication on their research was called "A Trip to 'Africa' in the New World." Right after returning from Suriname in 1928, MJH wrote to Ralph Linton, "the civilization of the Bush Negroes is much more African than anyone has dreamed," and to W. E. B. Du Bois, "Our trip to Suriname exceeded all my expectations. It is a rich culture there and a going concern that is almost completely African."

Going "Deepee"

> "We count it fortunate that we were able to penetrate the Suriname to its head, and farther, into the Pikien Rio, as far as there are any Bush-negro villages."

Herskovits arrived in Suriname with the firm belief that Bush Negroes would view Africa and things African as the deepest and most authentic aspects of their own culture, representing their most dangerous and powerful domain and the most difficult for the ethnographer to penetrate. Kahn told MJH before they set out together in 1928:

> Their every day language is the usual "Talkee, talkee" of the colony. They have, however, a ceremonial language which is called "Deepee talkee," which means "Deep talk". In this they tell of the Rebellion of 1750, the chief incidents and battles and names of the leaders who led them to their freedom. I was told by men of long residence in the colony, who are familiar with the bush negro, that the "Deepee talkee" language consists mostly of modified African words.

The idea that Bush Negroes had a two-level culture—one consisting of a kind of "spurious culture" presented to outsiders as a protective screen, the other of deep, secret, African realities—was part of the received wisdom among educated, urban Surinamers and those few outsiders who had written about them.

Indeed, this view was still common in the 1960s, when Thomas J. Price, one of MJH's last Ph.D. students at Northwestern, conducted brief fieldwork among the Aluku Maroons (to the east of the Saramakas) and devoted much of an article to their "resistance to ethnographic probing" and their ideas about Africa.

> The term "Dipi" may be applied to anything which should not be revealed. In order to retain their cultural privacy...[they] have made a high art of institutionalized prevarication. The mastery of the art of indirection and of giving misleading but logical answers is shared by all members of the society.... In dealing with outsiders, one set of terms for villages, rivers, ritual objects, and the like, are employed, another set when speaking to one another. In a sense, a layer of spurious culture has, through the years, been created to shield [Bush Negro] custom from the outside world.... A general knowledge of African cultures is invaluable to a researcher. [They] are exceedingly interested in Africa.... On the one hand, such knowledge generates the suspicion that the foreigner knows more about local custom than is actually the case. On the other hand...the anthropologist's acquaintance with African backgrounds raises his status above that of an ordinary bakra.

The notion that among Bush Negroes the anthropologist's knowledge of Africa raises his status was central to the Herskovitses' field strategy. "The Bakra said he knew something about Africa. The Ashanti people, for instance were a fine people," or "The Bak'a knows the land of the Negroes—*a sabi*

Afrika," exclaim the Saramakas of MJH, or again, "[Saramakas] said,...'You must have strong obia from Africa—strong snake obia—for the gods to have spoken so well of you!'." And the Herskovitses write, in a passage which presumes that their presence is at the very center of Saramaka concerns, that MJH's knowledge of Africa is the heart of his fame: "From boat to boat, from boat to shore, from shore to village the news went." "It was also whispered among our men that the Bakra's magic from Africa—a wholly imaginary thing, but which explained to the Bush Negroes our ability to do or withstand things that were not expected of us—had something to do with it, too."

From first to last, the Herskovitses' encounters with Saramakas were heavily mediated by outsiders— scientific colleagues, guides, cooks, informants and interpreters from the city—all of whom spoke English and accepted the received wisdom about Bush Negroes as a people harboring large stores of African-derived secrets which they would go to great lengths to protect. R. M. Schmidt, the English-speaking Christian Saramaka schoolteacher, shared many of these outsiders' "educated" views (even referring to his own people as "Djukas" when speaking to Herskovits). For example, MJH wrote excitedly on his fifth day in Saramaka territory, that

> [Schmidt] told me yesterday concerning the carved motifs on the woodwork that they have meanings, that the Djukas do not like to reveal it, and that while he doesn't know it he believes it has a sexual

connotation when given by a man to a woman. They certainly won't tell.

(Until the middle of the twentieth century, urban Surinamers used the term "Djuka" to refer generically to Bush Negroes/Maroons, though these latter considered the term pejorative and preferred to be called by the names of their specific groups—Saramakas, Aucaners/Ndyukas, Alukus, and so forth. In their publications, the Herskovitses always wrote of "Saramakas," but throughout his field diaries, MJH referred to the people they were interacting with as "Djukas," adopting the term of his city guides and servants.)

In their 1930 article on art, the Herskovitses repeated their idea that Bush Negroes were evasive about the meanings of their artistic symbols because they relate to deep and dangerous domains—allegedly, fertility and the gods—that only a specialized form of questioning would allow the outsider to penetrate.

Moravian schoolteachers gathered for a conference in Paramaribo, 1927
R. M. Schmidt is present but we are unable to pick him out of the crowd

Analysis of [Bush-Negro art] is impossible without the assistance of the natives, and the natives have an engaging way of evading the questions of the investigator when appealed to for the meanings of the carvings. Some of this evasion may be traced to the African's love of strategy though, in the main, there is a more direct factor. These carvings given to women by men have a sex symbolism which dominates most of the art, and, since this symbolism is related to the concept of fertility not alone of the women, but also of the fields and of the forest and the game animals which inhabit it, it is dangerous to offend the spirits by speaking too freely of these matters.

Whatever the psychological motives, the Bush-Negro is ingenious in eluding his questioner. He will say that the carving is of wood; he will name the wood it is made of; he will say it is beautiful; that it is an "in and out" design; he will say it is carpentry, or that it is done with a knife, or that it is decoration, to name a few of the recurrent answers. The fact is that we were entirely unsuccessful in obtaining a single explanation of design during our first visit to these people, and we count it sheer good fortune that brought to our camp early during our second expedition a young man with one of the crudest stools we had seen on the river. We bought the stool and it is from him that we learned enough to guide our future questioning.

A close reading of MJH's diary suggests that "our future questioning" often consisted of MJH persuading a reluctant Saramaka of the "meaning" of a piece, using a critical vocabulary which he himself had

created and which he then offered to informants as a
prod for further stories of the sort he had in mind. For
example, he once "took off a rubbing of the top and
sides of a bangi [stool].... On the side, was the plainest
snake-design I've seen yet, and even the maker
admitted it!" Or, discussing a carved paddle,

> "There are two snakes," we said, pointing to
> the realistically entwined bodies...ending at the top
> with recognizable heads, and with mouths held
> open, which supported symmetrical figures of the
> top of the paddle.
> "Aboma snakes," one man said, verifying to
> himself our statement.
> "These," we continued, "are the teeth of the
> great lizard—*bamba tande*—and this part...is a
> carved chain, and you call it *moni mo' muye*—money
> is more than woman."
> The men laughed. "Awa, so it is. The man
> knows about Saramacca carving."

We think it significant that the vocabulary of
symbolism "discovered" by the Herskovitses came
almost exclusively from the "young man with one of
the crudest stools we had seen on the river" who
approached them for a sale. Amonika or Tutú (called
Bayo in *Rebel Destiny*) was a most unusual Saramaka
twenty-one-year-old, for he had absolutely no compe-
tence in woodcarving (though he is portrayed as
unusually clever, ambitious about earning money, and
familiar with whitefolks). In *Rebel Destiny*, Bayo's lack
of skill as a woodcarver is portrayed through a conversation with his aunt:

"Will Bayo be married before we leave the bush?" we asked....

Bayo's aunt laughed...when she heard the question....

It seemed that Bayo had...to see to many things before he could marry. He had not yet...made any of the carvings which he needed to give his betrothed and her mother, for Bayo was a poor carver.

"Bayo has cunning in his eyes, and his head, but his fingers have no cunning, Bak'a."...

Before he was married...Bayo would have to see to the carvings which a man had to have for marrying.

"I do not like to carve. But I have friends who will carve for me while I go hunting for them!"

"Bayo" served as one of the Herskovitses' canoemen and by far their most frequently used Saramaka informant on their trips to the village of the chief and the Sara Creek. Our readings of MJH's field-notes suggest that he was particularly quick to catch on to what the anthropologists wanted to hear, and that he gave it to them over and over again.

MJH's 1929 diary records, "I went over some pictures of last year's specimens with Tutú and got their interpretation, and also worked out the symbolism of some of this year's pieces." In *Rebel Destiny* this moment is imaginatively expanded:

Bayo could take up many of our photographs of pieces...and describe the symbols to us which made up the carvings...."This and this are women, and these are men. A man and woman to one side, and a man and woman facing them."...The small designs close to the rim of the tray, facing each other, were the children to be born of these unions.

"This is a boy, and this a girl. That is for both women to make twins."

MJH with Saramaka artifacts (Northwestern University, 1929)
Photo John D. Jones

We were looking over his shoulder as he
explained the symbols, but still could not distin-
guish in the symbols to the side which represented
the male child and which the female.

Bayo laughed. "All this isn't easy, white man. A
line about this curve shows this to be a man-child.
These are things bush people alone know."...
The design...was divided into four parts, the cross-
hatched portion alternating with that of checkered
squares. Did those have meaning? we asked Bayo.

"Ai, these belong to the women and the children. The small lines are the hair of the children,
and the squares here that of the women." The
brass-headed nails he touched one by one on the
photograph. "The women have nice kamemba"
[cicatrizations], he said, at last.

No doubt, the idea that there was a secret
layer of culture among Bush Negroes, waiting for the
persistent anthropologist to uncover, conforms to a
general "Heart of Darkness" paradigm—the penetra-
tion of a deep interior that was so important to
Victorian explorers, wild-game hunters, collectors,
anthropologists, and others. We are struck, nonetheless, by the way the Herskovitses accepted this model
uncritically, conducted their fieldwork in terms of it,
and used it in their publications to portray both the
anthropologists and the descendants of rebel slaves as
heroes. And the way this model, or mind-set about the
people they were studying, contributed to their
growing anxieties about not learning enough—and
about learning far too much.

A Wife in the Field

"If Mrs. Herskovits accompanies us, I think it
would be distinctly inadvisable for her to go up the
river.... There is no use trying to mince words,—
going up the river is a hard and physically trying
experience, and I do not consider it at all the type
of trip that a woman should undertake."
(Morton C. Kahn, 1927)

As soon as an expedition to Suriname was conceived,
special concerns were voiced by MJH and others
about the comfort and safety of FSH. Even plans for
the voyage were subject to prevailing notions about
what hardships women should be exposed to. Kahn
wrote Herskovits about why they would not be able to
travel on a particular ship: "They have suitable
arrangements for male passengers on these freight
boats but Allen is somewhat adverse to having Mrs.
Herskovits as a passenger.... I have been informed that
it is absolutely contrary to the laws of the Company to
include women as super-cargoes on their boats."

Herskovits made claims to being liberal, for
his time, in his views of a woman's place; on the
voyage, he treated disparagingly a honeymooning
American woman who was against "woman's suffrage"
and who acquiesced complacently when her husband
remarked that "A wife's place is to help her husband."
But he also took seriously his responsibility for
protecting his wife from the dangers and discomforts
that he anticipated in the field. Before setting out on
their first expedition, and considering whether FSH

should accompany him upriver, MJH took his cues from Kahn, who advised,

> Speaking very frankly, the trip would be quite diffi-cult for Mrs. Herskovits. The rivers are infected with considerable pernicious malaria, to say nothing of yaws, biting insects of several kinds, and the hardships one has to put up with from the terrific heat, rough food, thorough wettings and other uncomfortable exigencies of river travel. Shooting the rapids is a dangerous stunt, and there is no use in trying to fool oneself in this regard.

But MJH still wondered whether FSH couldn't accompany them as far as the village of Gansee, where there was a Moravian mission, and stay there to work while they continued upriver. Herskovits to Kahn:

> I realize, of course, that going into the Bush country is no picnic and while, after reading your letter, I should not want Frances to go into the back country, I see no reason why she should not be able to do work at Gansee.... There is a Moravian mission there...[and] a Dutch lumber factor who lives not far from the village. Would his presence make her staying at the village more secure?

Kahn's reply was unambiguous:

> If it were my wife, sister or sweetheart I should not, by any means, take her to that country. The lumber factor, of whom I spoke, at Gansee as well as the

Moravian missionary at the same place are negroes, and while I do not think any real danger would result from Mrs. Herskovits' visit...one can never tell what happens in the backwoods communities.

Morton C. Kahn, M.D. (1937)

Herskovits accepted the advice: "I think we will work according to your suggestions leaving Frances at Paramaribo while we go into the interior." But the two men continued to think about assuring Frances' safety. At Herskovits' mention that an army captain had offered to show her how to use a pistol, Kahn replied,

> I think it an excellent plan that both of you learn to use firearms.... I would be glad to send Mrs. Herskovits my little automatic if it were not for the Sullivan law in this state, which prohibits any such procedure. I am sure the army post would have a .25 automatic Colt similar to the one in my possession.

Diary entries from their trip indicate that they took care of getting permits for their guns on the morning of their first full day in Paramaribo.

Special concern for FSH's safety continued to pepper Herskovits' letters and diary entries both during her solo stay in Paramaribo in 1928 and on their joint 1929 trip upriver. "There will be a [winti] dance on the Queen Mother's birthday, and [Fann] may be able to go [accompanied by Duffy's mother]. But not unless it is safe, of course." And in a pre-field-work letter to Rogalli: "I shall be very happy to have [Bundel] go with us in the bush as I have confidence in him and, since Mrs. Herskovits is going along, I feel that every safeguard should be taken to make her trip comfortable and safe."

Compared with her husband, Frances Herskovits experienced very few health problems, but when she did they were interpreted in terms of a delicate constitution. Soon after they arrive in Saramaka territory and witness coffin divination ("we took plenty of citronella, for the stench was pretty bad"), Fann develops a fever of 102° and they conclude that it's "the shock of what we saw yesterday...the ceremony of questioning was too much for her, we think." In contrast, MJH's own recurring bouts of fever, headaches, sore throat, rashes, infected boils, painful pimples, and more are seen as straightforward physical conditions, to be treated by bed rest, doctors' lancings and physics, and a variety of medicines brought to the field for emergencies.

FSH's notebooks reveal very little about her attitude toward all this (though MJH did report in a letter to Kahn, "I explained all the horrors to Frances and they did not feaze her a bit"). It is clear from numerous remarks in MJH's diary and field notes, however, that she was no shrinking violet, and that she took to the role of fieldworker with relish. And that, despite her lack of formal training in anthropology, she was—in terms of gathering first-hand ethnographic data during their summers in Suriname—the more productive of the two.

As we've seen, she was interviewing successfully within days of their arrival in Suriname (while her husband was sick in bed), and MJH makes frequent admiring allusions to her continuing feats as a fieldworker, contrasting it each time to his own frustrations:

> [In the village of Seei, the women] swarmed about Fann, incidentally giving her much information....

[On their first full day in the chief's village:] Fann has already started with the women, but I haven't seen much of the men as yet.... Fann is getting on well with the women—She got a full account of widowhood & menstrual customs and some religious information, but I sat in krutus [council meetings] and listened while Wolff wrote letters to the Governor.... Fann works excellently with the women.... What with krutus and a scarcity of men, I'm having a hard time.... In the afternoon I tried to get information from the Ga-ma, but wasn't very successful, but Fann got stunning stuff about the birth of twins from the women.

Part of the reason for FSH's greater success as an ethnographer was the linguistic head-start she had from her 1928 Paramaribo research, which was conducted mainly in Sranan-tongo, the creole language of coastal Suriname. Because of the strong grammatical parallels between Saramaccan and Sranan-tongo (a language that would have been more or less understood by most of the Saramaka men with whom they interacted), it is relatively easy to introduce Saramaccan words into Sranan-tongo sentences, gradually increasing them as familiarity with the language builds. In contrast, MJH had used English for the interviews with van Lier, Wolff, Rogalli, Bundel, Duffy, and Schmidt that constituted the great bulk of his 1928 Saramaka ethnography. And his 1929 encounters with Saramakas were almost always mediated by men who spoke English (Wolff, Schloss, Schmidt); he was almost never "taken off" by a group of Saramakas for animated conversations the way FSH often was.

To Saramakas, however, the most interesting gender issues raised by the Herskovitses' arrival had nothing to do with notions of female fragility or linguistic ability, but rather with dress. MJH's diary makes frequent mention of the lively comments that FSH's pants and boots inspired at villages up and down the river, and Saramakas' skepticism that it was a woman inside them. Her gear had in fact been put together on the basis of advice from Kahn and others, and was designed for protection against the dangers of the deep interior. (MJH, too, had assembled his outfit with care; stopping in Port-au-Prince on the 1928 voyage south: "We walked to the store where...I was to get a sun-helmet.... My helmet is a peach,—thick but light, with a long extension behind that should protect my neck.... It only cost $7, as against the $16 that Abercrombie & Fitch wanted.") Saramakas' reaction to FSH's clothes went directly into *Rebel Destiny*:

> From the provision grounds canoes filled with women would dart toward us, and Bayo would call to us, as the women cried their greetings, "Stand up, both of you. The women want to look at you."
>
> ...Hurriedly we would climb out from inside the tent and balance ourselves on our knees over the tarpaulin-covered load in front of the boat.
>
> "Look! Look!—there are two men! It is not true that the white man brought his woman!"
>
> Like a master showman, Bayo would stand there in the bow...all his teeth showing.
>
> "Take off your sun helmet, white woman," he would then say.
>
> "Mother of all Negroes!"...

"Is it that way they live in the white man's
country? Do they not know the difference between
men and women, that they both dress alike?"

Ethnographic Fairytales

"[In the Suriname interior] the use of informants in
the conventional sense was not possible.
Information could be obtained in two ways only—
by chance observation of actual happenings, and by
discussing specific events as they entered into
conversations with individual Bush Negroes."

There was an uncomfortable tension in MJH's mind
between what he thought anthropological fieldwork
should be and the way his Saramaka research was
progressing. In his diaries he often tweaked daily realities lightly toward his ideal, but in *Rebel Destiny* (and
other publications) he and FSH transformed them
wholesale. The contrasts between the fieldnotes and
the published depictions are revealing, for they attest,
implicitly, to the strength in 1920s American anthropology of an ideal of the ethnographer single-hand-
edly discovering, among larger-than-life natives, the
deep secrets of an exotic culture. They attest as well to
the Herskovitses' firm empiricist assumption that
ethnography consists of the epistemologically uncom-
plicated task of "collecting data" (the facts, just the
facts). And they bear witness to the couple's unques-
tioning conformity to the colonial practices of their
time and place.

During his first summer in Wolff's camp, MJH dreams of realizing his fieldwork utopia:

> It's an ethnological gold-mine here.... If I come back...I'll want to go to a village with Fann—not at a camp outside, as I am here,—and stay there at least six weeks, and just make friends and keep my eyes open. And then I'd get loads of data. It's here so thick it will take a steam-shovel to gather it in.

And as soon as their joint Saramaka research is over, he writes as if they had.

> From the point of view of ethnographic field method, the advantage of being able to live in a native village is inestimable. The opportunity of witnessing the daily routine of the life of a people being studied is attained only when the ethnologist's presence has become sufficiently a matter of course to allow the natives to go about their tasks without becoming unduly disturbed by a stranger being about.... This was fully the case during our stay in the bush.

This image has the lone anthropologist (or anthropological couple) working in the native language and depending on a combination of formal interviewing and interactions with the natives as they go about their normal lives. Cultural intermediaries (Western-oriented, Christian natives) are absent, as are interpreters, guides, and other servants brought in from the city.

Yet during their time in the field, the Herskovitses largely conformed to the colonial model for white visitors traveling among the natives, and these practices strongly affected the production of knowledge in their case. As MJH's diaries make clear over and over, he (and later they) were surrounded throughout their time in the field by an entourage of non-Saramakas who were paid both for menial jobs like cooking, washing, and cleaning, and for the great bulk of their information about Saramaka life and culture. And it is these people (along with MJH's key informant, a Saramaka Christian schoolmaster) who are, to a startling extent, simply "disappeared" in the publications.

The Herskovitses take pains to stress that *Rebel Destiny* "is not an ethnographic treatise," promising that "the scientific discussion of these data will appear in monographic form" (though that promise was never fulfilled). But they also insist that "nothing has been included either in descriptive detail, in the spoken or unspoken thoughts attributed to a Bush Negro, or in characterization, which has not been given us by our Bush Negro informants or has not been witnessed by ourselves." In other words, while the intent of the book is (in MJH's words) "literary rather than...scientific"— one critic characterizes it as "romantic relativism"—the facts are vouchsafed to be "true" and derived either from Bush Negro informants or personal observation.

Consider the following accounts of the Herskovitses' arrival in the village of the chief—the first from MJH's diary, and the second from *Rebel Destiny*.

The old fellow [Granman Djankuso] is a big man
and he is obviously very friendly with Wolff. We
went to his own official meeting place, where we
are to sleep,—Schloss has a house, Jacoba slings
with the Wolffs across the way, there's a cook-
house, and a tiny little house where we can rest.

After a silence, the Granman spoke. "...I have set
aside five houses for the Bak'a.... The Bak'a and his
woman will put up their hammocks here. Here they
will stay. The white man's goods are stored in the
house in back of mine.... There is a man from the
city who helps them. He will sleep where these
goods are stored.... The house in back of this I have
had the women get ready also for the white man
and his woman.... I have given a house for the cook,
and an open house for the cooking."

The elisions here are subtle but telling. The
diaries reveal that, from the beginning of his first
summer in Saramaka, until this arrival at the village of
the chief near the end of the second, Herskovits had
spent but five days (when he was traveling on the river
with Rogalli) outside the presence of Wolff. Because
of Wolff's frequent dealings with the chief, the
Herskovitses considered it essential that he accompany
them upstream to speak on their behalf and act as
interpreter, so they paid his trip, and he took advan-
tage of what he saw as a jaunt to bring along his
woman and her children.

According to MJH's diary, the Herskovits
party set out in four canoes carrying Wolff, his "cook"
and her children, Fred and Jacoba (employed by the

Herskovitses as cook and maid respectively but used frequently as informants about Saramaka culture), and Schloss, their experienced "bush guide" who stayed with them during every step of their 1929 expedition. (Several days into the trip, Fred fell ill and was sent back.) In the published version of their upriver trip and stay in the chief's village, the presence of Wolff, his companion, and the children is simply erased—the anthropologists appear only with a female cook and "a man from the city who helps them." (And in a particularly cheeky transformation, MJH depicts himself in *Rebel Destiny* reading out loud, at the chief's request, a letter written to the chief by "a lumber factor down the river," but his diary records that the lumber factor—Wolff, the Herskovits' cicerone in the chief's village—was the one reading letters for the chief and taking his dictation.)

An even more revealing elision concerns R. M. Schmidt, the man MJH described categorically in 1929 as "my best informant." As he wrote the year before, "Schmidt, the school-master at Gansee, [is] a Djuka-born native who speaks good English." Later: "He knows the culture of the Bush Negroes exceedingly well, is a good interpreter and a highly intelligent man, and I feel privileged to have been able to work with him." Herskovits wrote several letters to make special arrangements (via the Colonial Secretary and the Director of the Moravian Mission) to have Schmidt get leave from his job and meet him upon his arrival in Paramaribo in 1929, where they immediately began interviews on a wide range of subjects, taking up where they had left off the previous summer. Once at Wolff's base camp, the Herskovitses had Schmidt take them around—he was the first to escort them to a village, pointing things out, explaining as they went, and he then sat down for a number of formal interviews with MJH as well as, separately, with FSH on such subjects as menstrual practices. Even on their penultimate day before heading toward Paramaribo, Herskovits conducted a long, formal interview with him. Yet, in all of the Herskovitses' many publications about Saramaka, Schmidt's existence is acknowledged only twice: once in a technical article on social organization, and once in *Rebel Destiny*, where readers are told that Schmidt merely provided contacts with the natives. Elsewhere, he is systematically erased.

Replacing this missionary-schoolmaster as "best informant" in the published work is young "Bayo." Several chapters are devoted to him in *Rebel Destiny* (Bayo as "playboy," Bayo as "obia-man"), there are two photos of him, and his cultural knowledge is extolled. But while he was probably the non-Christian Saramaka most willing to speak with the Herskovitses, MJH's diaries mention him far less frequently than Schmidt (or, for that matter, Wolff or even van Lier).

Schmidt represented precisely the kind of Saramaka informant on whom MJH was least eager

"Bayo inspects an Obia leaf."

to admit dependence. A Christian (and, hence in the eyes of many on the river, not a "real") Saramaka, and an educated, influential schoolmaster at the Moravian school in Gansee about to be appointed headmaster of the large school on the coast at Moengo, he spoke good English and later read MJH's publications with interest. Like W. F. van Lier, the authority on Ndyuka ethnography, Schmidt was far too educated and Westernized to represent the image of the native informant the Herskovitses wished to portray in the deep interior of Suriname. The precise wording of the joint acknowledgment in *Rebel Destiny* to the three men—Schmidt, van Lier, and Wolff—who, collectively, gave MJH the better part of the Bush Negro ethnography he published, cannot be dismissed as innocent: "for their great help in making contacts for us with the natives with whom we worked."

Like much anthropological writing of the day, the Herskovitses' published depictions artificially isolate their people's territory from the outside world. The active mining, logging, and missionizing that was taking place in Saramaka during the time they were there and the ongoing political struggles between the colonial government and Saramaka authorities go largely unremarked. For example, MJH's diary records that "there was a Catholic priest [aboard the train] going up to the head of the Suriname River to his mission who had a long and hot argument with Rogali about the iniquity of the Moravians and their missions." Indeed, Father Morssink, who had his missionpost among the Saramakas even deeper into the interior than the Herskovitses ever reached, and

W. F. van Lier, upon his appointment as government pos"older among the Ndyuka, 1918

whose knowledge of Saramaka life in many ways surpassed that of the anthropologists, had already baptized a number of people in the downstream village of Lombé (where MJH made the bulk of his 1928 "African" discoveries). And MJH's and Kahn's friend Captain Abaisa of Lombé had been pressing the priest ever since 1918 to build a church there. Moreover, during the 1920s, Saramaka relations with the colonial government were often stormy; government official L. Junker (who wrote a number of articles about Saramaka society in scholarly journals during the period) engaged in fierce and public battles of wills with Granman Djankuso. Yet in their publications, the Herskovitses make almost no mention of Catholic missions in Saramaka or relations between the chief and the colonial government, instead adopting the perspective that MJH expressed in an early letter to Kahn: "It is a sort of ethnological Paradise, as far as I can see,—plenty of work in a field almost untouched."

Fears, Illness, and the Unknown

> "The two new boils that developed were
> ripening—and sitting on two boils for eight hours
> is no joke."

The Herskovitses were urbane and cultured: MJH reported experiencing "the thrill of my life" when the Victrola in the sitting room of their Paramaribo hotel began playing the Tchaikovsky B-flat minor piano concerto, and FSH commended Rogalli for saying, "If I could take a good piano into the bush, I'd take it. There's no use making life harder than it is." And Walter Jackson describes FSH ("a New Yorker with literary ambitions who had spent a few months in Paris as an expatriated but unpublished writer") and MJH as frequenting, during the mid-1920s in New York, a circle of friends with whom they "discussed music, avant-garde art, literature, feminism, and politics—reveling in its cosmopolitan ambiance, and sharing its generational revolt against Babbittry."

But they were inexperienced travelers. Preparations for going to the deep bush brought understandable anxieties. Before leaving for Suriname, MJH exchanged letters with experts such as Morton Kahn in New York and L. C. van Panhuys in the Netherlands and received an earful about potential health hazards.

> It will be nearly impossible to study Bush negroes
> and not to be bitten in the same time by mosqui-
> toes, infected with Bushnegro-blood, viz. with

malaria-plasm[—?—]. If you could remain after sunset in your mosquito-free tent, you could remain free from the plague, but as it is necessary for you to study/visit them also in the evening and in their cabins, you will be infected. Therefore you will have to take quinine.... You can protect yourself by wearing <u>gloves</u>, and...<u>underclothes</u>, <u>not</u> too thin, and f.i. <u>high</u> boots, with a leathern tongue, very broad (in order that the fore part of your foot is always protected).

After he and FSH received their various inoculations and bought their bush equipment, including a revolver for her, they set off on their adventure.

It is hard to know whether anxieties about his first foreign fieldwork had anything to do with MJH's nearly daily diary jottings about his bodily ills, but it doesn't take a psychoanalyst to suspect that they might have. Here, in his own words, is some of what he was experiencing—first, on the 1928 voyage to Suriname:

[27 June] All morning long we've been going by the coast of Haiti.... My leg bothered me—I'm developing what seems to be a boil, something I probably made worse by squeezing it and trying to open it.... My leg is very angry. Hard, and a large red spot about the boil that looks bad. The doctor ordered me to bed with a wet dressing. [30 June] The infection is down but the boil hasn't opened. All Thursday I was in bed and most of yesterday.... We got on our helmets, drank our two glasses of water apiece, and went ashore [at Curaçao].... But my leg began rampaging, so I returned to the boat.... Then to bed with dressings again. [3 July]

I've become thoroughly acquainted with two bunks. The Doctor lanced my boil Sunday,—a bloody proceeding, but not painful since he froze it first. Then the fun began.... When my bed began to look partly bloody the dressing was changed. That was about six o'clock. About eight, the wound began bleeding pretty badly. Poor Fann!—she felt it awfully, but I imagined that the bleeding was in order, and restrained her till nine. Then she determined to wait no longer [and]...the steward called the Doctor.... Apparently, the toxins had induced a haemophilia, and they wasted no time stopping the flow. [FSH's own diary entry for that Sunday remarks "They stopped the bleeding at 11. We both took a shot of cognac—Mel a double one."]...

Yesterday the wound was closed tight so the [—?—] had a chance to stew[?] and my side began to pain me so the Doctor opened it again and this time it behaved and oozed a slow steady discharge that relieved me a lot. And all night it continued.

...I'm sitting in a deck-chair in the room, much more comfortable than before, a wet dressing promises to persuade the core of the boil out, and I should be at last on the mend. [6 July] I had my leg dressed; it's getting steadily better. [8 July] My foot gets steadily better—for which many thanks!

After their arrival in Suriname on July 10, the problems continue:

[11 July] There was a terrific downpour last night, and I turned out to close the windows, got wet, and got up this morning with a sore throat that travelled down my bronchial tubes as the day wore on. In the morning I went back to the Cottica to have my wound dressed.... [In the evening] I got a shock when I undressed. For I had a rash all over my body! Hell!! [12 July] I showed my complication to Kahn this morning and he thought it might be prickly-heat but we called a doctor anyway.... In the afternoon...I was feeling groggy—the doctor had given me a wash and a physic. [13 July] My face, I'm afraid will be a sight for the Governor today, swollen and blotched and my head feels filled with cotton. But the rash seems no worse. The only development is a sore throat.... The physic had[—?—]out my tummy badly, and so we went to the military hospital. Dr. Lambert looked me over decided it wasn't prickly-heat but a skin affection (maybe due to the quinine, heaven help me) and called in a young specialist, very nice...and told me to take it easy, gargle faithfully, and come back before I ventured into the bush. They gave me an injection of adrenaline that palped my heart, temporarily lightening the rash.

I rested in the afternoon... [by evening] I was burning all over—102° as it later proved, so I finally gave in and went to bed, where I tossed and tossed. [17 July] And in bed I stayed until this morning. And I'm weak as a cat.... Black buzzards and green tomcats! It's enough to make strong men weep!

...Altho just what I have and why I have it is a mystery, I'm better. They thought food, and kidneys, and finally settled on maybe a strepto-coccic infection from my leg which became general and went to my skin and throat. Anyhow, whatever it is, it got me good and plenty. [18 July] Delighted to be a bit stronger, altho the rash still persists. But though I'm still weak, I don't feel ill as I did ever since I got here. I ventured out in the world for the first time, going to the hospital to be looked over. [20 July] Before dinner I had a cocktail and half of Fann's, and after dinner my temp walked up to 38.1° C—so I went to bed for a restless night. I guess "veesky soda" is my limit these days. [24 July] The trip [by train] was hot.... My feet began to itch a bit from the boots and when I took them off there were huge welts that itched—sort of hives or aggravated prickly-heat. Rogalli made me keep from scratching it and I rubbed it with a bit of orange, a local remedy which, I can testify, is efficacious. Aside from a slight headache from the heat and not eating enough, I've stood the trip excellently. [25 July, after the first night at the base camp] We are very fortunate—no anopheles. Last night we sat around and weren't bitten at all. But the 10 grains a day of quinine prophylactically stays in order just the same. [26 July] A bad pimple on what R[ogali] calls the "codex" sums up the disabilities—nothing serious tho, on my part, it makes the sitting somewhat painful.... I was restless due to that damned new big pimple. [27 July] My pimple busted, and I feel much better. Others will probably replace them, but if I get off with nothing worse I'll sing a <u>Gloria</u>. [1 August] The two new boils that developed were ripening—and sitting on two boils for eight hours is no joke. They broke open as camp was established and that relieved them a lot. [4 August] By that time we were at the water's edge, I had stowed away my purchases and washed my hands with antiseptic soap and we were off down the river.

During the second summer, MJH suffered less, though there are periods when illness and attendant anxieties again come to the fore. Three days after arriving at their base camp from Paramaribo, he writes, "I woke up about 8 o'clock with a splitting headache, and wondering what I might be getting. But with Peramydon[Pyramidon] it passed away, leaving nothing worse than the itch of red-bugs, which are plaguing both of us" and the very final page of the diary reports: "I got up feeling wretched; the cold that's been somewhat in the offing ever since Asindopo matured, and I had a racking cough and felt rather woozy." In between, he worries about Fann's health too: "Up feeling rather tired, and soon after Fann called. She was dizzy, and pale, but no fever until later. I was afraid of malaria and she had 10 grams [of quinine] at 8, 12, and 6—a heroic dose.... I gave her a sleeping-tablet.... The fever holds steady, between 100° and 102°." Notations on the final page of MJH's field notebook show that between 8 AM and 5:20 PM that day, he took Fann's temperature twelve times (with the highest reading 101.4°), registered her pulse (which ranged between 84 and 93) eight times, and recorded her respiration three times. His diary adds: "I took some castor oil as a precautionary measure."

FSH, who almost never mentioned her own health in her diaries, was deeply concerned about her husband's frequent sufferings. On 12 July 1928, for example, she wrote: "Worried about Mel. He seems to catch everything that's to be caught." Four days later, she reported: "Mel's depressed. He burst out into sobs because a confounded tango was being played again and again. We've taken away the record and stored it inside the night table." Occasionally she adopts a sentimental tone—on the day he took the train into the bush, she wrote: "Stood at the window watching the sunset, watching the moon, imagining things—Mel on the river, Mel crossing the falls, Mel at Gansee.—This same moon is illumining for him...what?"

MJH's feelings about being "alone"—that is, without other whites—surface early in their trip, as the Cottica puts in at Port-au-Prince and they debark for a stroll on the Grande Rue: "Negroes, negroes—scarcely ever a white face.... everywhere color, and a kind of sinister undercurrent that was hard to define but was perhaps only a sense of strangeness in ourselves." When Kahn is "alone" at Wolff's camp (with only his servants and Wolff), MJH muses that he "must be good and lonesome by now, up there in the bush with no one to talk to." And when, on Wolff's departure from the chief's village, MJH describes himself and Fann as being "alone in the interior," it is—as we shall see—with a strong sense of foreboding.

There were also more minor frights which fed Herskovits' nervousness in the field. On the third day at Wolff's camp, he "got a good scare back in the out-house—a spider came over the post as I opened the door, fully five inches across and heavy with black hair. It was as sinister a sight as I've ever seen, so I called Mort and let him kill it." And among MJH's companions from Paramaribo, a certain macho cama-raderie about the dangers of the bush went very much

with the territory. At Wolff's base camp, with Wolff,
Kahn, and Rogalli in attendance, he reports

> We sat and talked until half-past ten. Of shivery
> things—of the subtle poisons the Djuka knows, of
> the Aboma or boa-constrictor that lived in Wolff's
> house until a Djuka charmed him away with a
> string and soft words...of the different kinds of
> snakes and what happened to the children of the
> Djuka who killed one—of experiences in being
> caught in the bush, alone, at night.

The diaries make clear that throughout their 1929
voyage to the Suriname interior, the strangeness of the
environment, both human and physical, not only led
the Herskovitses to feel a real exhilaration about the
discoveries they were making, but also lent a sense of
constant edginess to their lives.

The Herskovitses had long imagined their projected
two-week stay in the chief's village as the climax of
their fieldwork, and as they passed village after village
on the upstream journey their feelings of anticipation
grew. (Until that moment, they hadn't been more than
overnight visitors in any Saramaka village.) From early
correspondence with Suriname experts, pointed interviews with Wolff, and details garnered from a number
of other informants they already had a picture of
Chief Djankuso's supreme stature as a political and
religious leader—more king than chief, and empow-
ered to grant or deny them access to his people and
their culture.

Preparations for their ceremonial arrival began while they were still several days downstream, and a high-ranking delegation was dispatched ahead of their boats to request formal permission for them to proceed. As they entered the Pikilio, guided by the pilot sent out by the chief, their canoemen fired a three-gun salute to announce their presence (answered by a similar salute from the chief's assistants on shore), and as they approached the landing place, boatloads of Saramakas paddled out to greet them with "much African hallooing from the women."

In the emotional buildup to their arrival at "the court of the granman," who would be surrounded by his "royal councillors," the Herskovitses were hoping that, at last, they might penetrate to the deepest core of Saramaka culture (which would perforce be its most authentically African layer). But tensions and anxieties heightened as they drew near. Would they finally be able to realize their ideal of fieldwork unmediated by interpreters and guides, participating almost unnoticed as Saramakas went about their everyday lives? Would Saramakas reveal their most powerful knowledge to them?

At long last, they were approaching "the true, true Saramacca country, the land which the Bush Negro feels to be entirely his own. White men, it is true, had been here before, but only a handful, and the gods of the river, who were powerful, saw to it that of these not many got back to the white man's land. True, true Saramacca country!"

High Anxiety

> "If they're afraid of what we learned, anything is
> possible; we're watching our food & water."

Concerns about MJH's career stood at the heart of
their anxieties that summer. (Kahn once chided him
for the "childish or kiddish attitude which you insist
on assuming...[which] makes you appear as a sort of
ruthlessly hyper-ambitious person.") His constant
attempts to reassure himself about the amount of
ethnographic knowledge he was "getting" left him
veering between grand confidence and extreme frus-
tration. FSH watched as tensions about their relationship with Saramakas mounted, and she gradually
developed a theory that played well in the light of
their joint concerns. Herskovits, she argued, was
learning so much about the people's most guarded
secrets and held such powerful knowledge of the
country of their ancestors that Saramakas felt seriously
threatened, at first simply causing them to hold back
further information, but eventually persuading them
to actually try to do the couple in.

Sometimes MJH expressed satisfaction about
his growing ethnographic knowledge and its promise
for his academic career. Only days after stepping off
the ship in 1928, he wrote that "plans for presentation
of the material I get began to shape themselves in my
mind. For the Congress, a paper in a sense a continua-
tion of Lindblom's 'Afrikanische Relikte,'—and for
[the journal] 'Africa,' a paper on the general problems

presented by the Negro in the New World.... I'm quite pleased with the way things are shaping up." Later he wrote, "I am increasingly confident that our results will be important and that we'll bring back significant material.... Wolff tells me he thinks I'm getting a great deal.... I certainly have enough for the two papers I envisaged,—and more." But by the second summer, he was often fretting about the pace of his learning: "I haven't seen much of the men as yet.... More krutus all day. I wonder when I'll have time to do any work.... What with krutus and a scarcity of men, I'm having a hard time.... In the afternoon I tried to get information from the Ga-ma, but wasn't very successful." To some extent, MJH's insecurities about his knowledge of Saramaka culture were balanced by a pride in his authority about Africa. But FSH's success at gathering information compared to his own, along with his wish to be supportive of her, seems to have left him feeling less than good about himself professionally during their upriver trip.

Herskovits' biographer described him as "confident when he was in full control of a situation, but sometimes insecure when he felt he was not." On his home turf among New York intelligentsia, he may have been (in Margaret Mead's words) "a bouncing, cheerful, unquenchable extrovert," but in Suriname, especially on the upriver trip to the chief's village, he seems to have been a man whose self-esteem frequently needed a boost. FSH—who was having an easier time of communicating with Saramakas, was gathering data with relative ease, and "tended to be more concerned about matters affecting Mel's career than he was"—stepped right in to shore it up. (But at the same time that she was flattering her husband's ego, might she also have been getting increasingly annoyed by his tendency to speak about subjects that should not have been addressed lightly—showing off about the sacred terms he knew, both African and Saramaka—which interfered on a number of occasions with their fieldwork? In the absence of diary entries on these issues in her hand, it's hard to know.) In any case, her efforts can be said to have backfired, building into the collective paranoia that marked the final days of their Saramaka fieldwork.

FSH began to develop her theory the day before they reached the chief's village, convincing MJH that his knowledge of the names of sacred dances had upset Saramakas so much that they cancelled a planned ceremony. The next morning,

> We were away by 7, and not sorry, for the village
> was not very friendly. Fann's hunch about naming
> dances being the cause of calling off the dance is, I
> believe, right, for they will dance tonight, and it is a
> ceremonial anniversary dance for a dead man. I
> mentioned Apukú, among others, and it seemed to
> startle people.

During the first two days in the chief's village, meetings are held to decide whether they will be welcome to stay for their planned two-week visit, and Herskovits feels guardedly optimistic, if still insecure: "I suppose we came thru all right.... They apparently approved of us." And the next day they have a productive session with the chief: "In the evening we sat with Wolff and the Gama.... He talked—and it was fascinating—until after nine."

But Fann continues to press her idea that the Saramakas are turning against them because MJH knows too much. MJH's optimism begins to erode under her growing sense of doom.

> I showed African pictures to the two Kapteins of Dahomey, and I thought they'd fall off their stools. The stuff is certainly making an impression—too much, I'm afraid, for today a woman who had been possessed in the morning promised to call us when the Gadu was in her and never did. Fann feels that the old fellow [the chief], for political reasons, is keeping things from getting to us, or at least not encouraging people. But I don't know,—anyway, we'll see.... In the evening W[olff] gave [liquor] for a dance, but it wasn't so hot—people came & drifted away again, and that strengthens our feeling.

The next day, FSH goes public with her feelings that Saramakas are blocking their work and has Wolff speak to the chief about it. In the pre-dawn hours they've heard village leaders murmuring in the council house immediately next to theirs, and without being able to understand what's being said they imagine the worst.

> Fann made it plain to [Wolff] that we were being blocked in our work and he talked to the old man.... Anyway, we're here for 9 or 10 days on our own, and we hope for the best.... A friend of Fann's

who told her the name of her gods became possessed this morning. When we saw her she was very nervous, and said she'd "play" in the evening and would call us. But nothing happened, and we suspect the worst.... I hope the royal councillors don't start tomorrow morning at 3 o'clock—it's a bit disturbing, more to Fann than to me.

Later that day, Wolff—who has fulfilled his responsibility for introducing the Herskovitses to the chief—departs back downstream with his family. Their first full day "on their own" (with only Schloss and Jacoba) is ethnographically rich, but they're still worrying about whether Saramakas trust them: "We went to...A Kissi a mau, across the river, and saw plenty.... The gadus have spoken—we saw 5 people have seizures and four of them said we came with good hearts." The next day the pressures continue to mount:

Grrr!, what a day. We went to two villages in the morning. It was a very cool reception.... Fann saw a circular house to Toné that they chased her away from and I didn't even see, and I wasn't even allowed to photograph shrines; especially the Kromanti house and another I later learned was to the papa-snake.... We came back in no pleasant mood.... In the afternoon I tried to get information from the Ga-ma, but wasn't very successful, but Fann got stunning stuff...from the women.... It's the damndest day we've had, and we're all at sixes & sevens.... So we'll try to sleep it off and hope that tomorrow will be better.

But it isn't.

> A worse day,—and an anxious one.... The old man
> has been making himself a little scarce these days—
> to talk & work. [Fann] wants to leave early; feels
> that we've gone so deeply into the religious and
> ceremonial life that we can get nothing more and
> that the old fellow is getting a bit uneasy. I wasn't
> sure—until later.

By afternoon, Fann decides the time has come
for action—she wants to leave—and MJH starts
accepting her vision of an impending threat to their
lives.

> We're alone in the interior, and Fann thinks my
> question of last night, when I mentioned the name
> of Ogun, the Nigerian god of war & iron, and
> whom they know, with Kromanti, which is
> undoubtedly their "standing army" and a secret
> society for protection, thoroughly alarmed them.
> What will happen no one can say, but we held a
> council of war and decided to act fast. We called
> the old chap in after supper and told him we'd
> promised the Governor that if anyone of us got
> sick, we'd leave, that we hated to but J[acoba] was
> more ill than I thought, and that I was no doctor,
> and tho we regretted it, we'd like to leave.... The
> larger number of men who are about, and the
> general atmosphere, are anything but reassuring....
> If they're afraid of what we learned, anything is
> possible; we're watching our food & water, and
> tomorrow Fann gets back into her boots.

They remain in the village one more day, as the chief makes arrangements for a boat to take them back. Although it is uneventful, they feel confirmed in their suspicions.

> Again an anxious day, but with the tension lighter toward the end. We woke up both of us tired after the night, with the 3 o'clock krutu that we could hear in murmurs but the intent of which we couldn't learn. So we had a shot of cognac and later took a sedative that quieted us somewhat. The women have been warned to keep quiet but be pleasant, so we had little to do but pack our trunks.... Certainly they think they've hoodwinked us on such matters as the name of the earth-mother and those of the lo, as well as on other matters.... After dinner we had another short krutu—two men and a woman, certainly workers of magic,—from Luango, were presented, and probably tried stunts afterwards.... After a very cool [unenthusiastic] Seketi dance, we went to sleep, and, by fastening the door and leaving the lantern lighted, we were able to sleep with a more comfortable feeling.

The next morning, Djankuso poses for MJH's camera, "putting on his white hat for the purpose" and, "After not too enthusiastic good-byes we left,...wondering if they'll try anything on the river."

Departure from the chief's village does not put an end to their perception of personal danger, however, and Fann's interpretation continues to fuel their anxiety. Two days downriver they hear one of their boatmen singing and construe the words to be an

MJH's photo of Chief Djankuso, 4 August 1929

invocation to "the Great God and the Yoruka [ances-
tral spirits]." They think they hear singing "about how
the Baka...should get out and how Fann's belly should
stop producing and that we all ought to die, it was
rather weird." And the next week, camping outside the
downstream village of Lombé, they "both imagine that
most of the people feel we're getting too much."

Getting Too Much?

> "I'm sure if they knew how much we really had it
> would go harder."

An assessment of FSH's interpretation of the hostility
they felt from Saramakas depends partly on an understanding of how Saramakas would have reacted to
MJH's engagements with their cultural "secrets." His
practice of photographing shrines and other cult
objects seems to have been tolerated in some instances
and to have caused a perfectly understandable irritation in others, but we strongly doubt it would have
produced much more than resentment. His request for
forest-spirit and other "sacred dances" at a "ceremonial anniversary dance" would have been seen by
Saramakas as off-the-wall rather than threatening. And
many of his pronouncements about African origins,
which were based on a combination of wishful
thinking and misunderstandings of Saramaka culture,
would simply not have been understood or much
mattered to them one way or the other.

For example, if MJH's assertion about Ogun and a Saramaka secret society had been communicated to Saramakas, they would certainly have reacted with puzzlement or curiosity rather than consternation. For, despite the undeniable richness of Saramaka cosmology, and its numerous links with deities from the African continent, there is no "Ogun" in their pantheon. (Nor is Ogun known to Ndyukas or Alukus.) Variants of this Nigerian god are present in much of the African diaspora, from Brazil through Cuba to New York, but not in the religion of "Bush Negroes." Herskovits' claim that the Saramaka "Kromanti" cult included Ogun, and that it constituted "their 'standing army' and a secret society for protection," could only have resulted from excessive zeal in seeking African connections, perhaps combined with his insisting on them in the presence of politely acquiescent Saramakas. (On the eve of the second summer's expedition, MJH had written, "I am hoping, too, that we will be able to learn whether there is any remnant of the African secret society present in the Bush-Negro culture. In view of the liveliness of the African elements in their culture, it seems strange that this all-important African aspect is not present.") He must have realized his mistake later, for the claim appears nowhere else in his diaries or notes and is totally absent from his publications.

The Herskovitses' conceit that Saramakas might kill them in order to protect cultural secrets bespeaks a rather poor understanding of local realities. They arrived in the chief's village with letters of intro-duction from the colonial governor and in the company of the chief's long-time friend, Wolff. It is true that Saramakas have always been suspicious of outsiders—indeed, if one were to establish an anthropological "scale for the intensity of distrust of outsiders," Saramakas would rank relatively high—but they haven't killed one since before their eighteenth-century peace treaty. Moreover, from a Saramaka perspective, the act of poisoning constitutes a crime that creates a merciless avenging spirit which lasts for generations.

During the Herskovitses' stay in the chief's village, Saramakas seem to have been acting with a perfectly understandable combination of cordiality and protectiveness about probings of their private space by the camera-bearing white man and his wife who, trousers notwithstanding, could easily have been bringing menstrual pollution dangerously close to their shrines. The chief treated them as honored guests, summoning one of the region's most renowned singers and dancers to perform for them, sending men out to hunt and fish for them, providing them with "I don't know how many kilos of rice and other things, and...a huge cut of venison," setting up excursions to neighboring villages, and even taking cutlass in hand to clear a special place for them to bathe in private. They were permitted to wander where they wanted, welcomed at various village events (from subsistence activities to funerals and possession dances), and generally tolerated as they took rubbings of carvings and photographs of local scenes. Many of the diary entries express real excitement, even on the most stress-ridden days, at the things they were discovering.

The times when Saramakas treated them with suspicion—for example, when a man whisked away the kaolin-smeared rattle that MJH had just "snapped" with his camera without asking permission—can certainly be said to go with the ethnographic territory.

The Herskovitses' diaries, field notes, and publications show that they touched on many aspects of Saramaka life during MJH's 17-day stay in 1928 and their joint six-week stay in 1929. When we consider how much of their time was spent sitting in a canoe, dealing with the logistics of the expedition, making sound recordings, and assembling two important museum collections, we can only be impressed that they learned as much as they did. Yet set against their own assessment of how much they'd gotten, their knowledge of Saramaka culture was meager. In terms of linguistic fluency, for example, they depicted themselves in *Rebel Destiny* as using "the clipped, rapid 'deep-Saramacca' speech" conversationally in the chief's village, and having difficulty with it only "when Bush Negroes spoke informally to one another," but the transcriptions they give in both field notes and publications (with frequent inclusion of 'r', a sound that does not exist in Saramaccan) are composed, with few exceptions, of words in Sranan-tongo, the native language of their city interpreter-guides and the language that FSH had used for her 1928 work in Paramaribo. (Morton Kahn is explicit about how Saramakas conducted themselves linguistically with whites: "When the Bush Negroes converse with outsiders they employ the talkee-talkee language which white men and Paramaribo Town Negroes can understand. But they also have a tribal language called...*Saramacca-tongo* known only among themselves.") The notion that the Herskovitses "knew too much" and had "gone too deep"—to the point of intruding so far into the most secret aspects of the culture that Saramakas might consider killing them—is, to put it mildly, unpersuasive. It is not too much to speak here of an ethnographically-rationalized paranoia.

The Servant Problem

"As a result we ate cold food for supper."

In late 2001, when we were reading the Suriname diaries and notes for the first time, the thing that most surprised us was the constant presence of the various people the Herskovitses had hired and the extent to which their fieldwork was mediated by them. Although we had long been familiar with their published work on Suriname, and had thus seen the mentions in *Rebel Destiny* of "our cook" and "our town man," we had no way of knowing that MJH was virtually never without either Rogalli, Bundel, Wolff, or Schmidt during the 1928 trip or that in 1929, aside from the moments when "Fann went off with the women," they were accompanied in all village visits by either Wolff, Schloss, or another paid guide. But what struck us even more forcefully than the presence of these buffers between the Herskovitses and Saramakas was the amount of time and psychic energy that MJH devoted to managing the people he'd hired, and the intense irritation that it caused him. As he wrote near the end of the second summer, "I'm fed up with the general supervision that takes my time."

Often the issue was money. It came up as early as the first week of the first summer when MJH heard through a mutual acquaintance that van Lier "wondered if he was to be paid for working with me." Herskovits reluctantly proffered ten guilders, and said he'd get some more later: "They're so damned round about, these people. And all Americans, of course, are millionaires. Gr-r-r!!" Numerous entries about his artifact collecting leave no doubt that he was a tough bargainer with Saramakas, haggling with determination, struggling against what he saw as their cupidity, and congratulating himself when he managed to pass trinkets off for money. During some bargaining for a carved stool, "Djukas appeared with their favorite phrase, 'Gi' me' on their lips"; or "I went out and got one of Woolworth's best red necklaces out of my sack.... My beads worked very well—they make up part of the price and save me that much." Money problems became even more irritating during the second summer, especially in terms of paying the boatmen, Wolff, Schloss, and Jacoba:

> Lalani said that since Gama kode is above the Saramacca in the Pikien Rio, they should have extra pay—four guilders a boat.... It is really outrageous, but I stalled and said I'd see, and when I told Fann she fumed!...about the extra fee. It is settled that I

shall pay two guilders a boat extra.... I consented on Wolff's advice.... But it made us angry.... I hope when we come to the big fellow [the chief] it will be the end, for those chaps are simply money-mad, and if Wolff weren't here I'd be in a difficult situation.—Too much civilisation, I'm afraid.... The [boat]men have not been nice—they ask and ask for everything, and spread stories in villages about how much we have.... Discovered the interesting fact that Wolff is staying several days at Abenastone to go into the bush—for which I shall not pay.

Sometimes the negotiations concerning payments lasted for hours. In a meeting with the chief about their return downstream,

we started, and talked & talked—4 solid hours. I offered f3.50 a day per man, but the old fellow wanted a price, so I agreed to give f28.00 a boat if they made it in 3 days—four day's pay. It took a lot of talk and I expected more, and we were all surprised when it was settled. Then there was a question of boat-hire, but I'm to give f3.00 per boat for the use of it—a hold-up if there ever were one.

But there were also other bones of contention between the Herskovitses and their hired help. In 1928, for example, MJH complained about Rogalli as interpreter because of his habit of diverting conversations to his favorite subjects of wood and crops. Or, "[Jacoba] has a tendency to quarrel & give orders, but some straight talking on my part to everyone in our party should put things to right." Or, "We won't have

*The Herskovitses' guide Schloss (right) with a man
we believe to be Lalani (Lombé, 1929)*

many more days of travelling, fortunately, for it is very hard and trying, and the Lombé [boat]men are always making trouble." Or again, "Schloss and Jacoba made me furious with their inefficiency and I caught a good headache."

During the first four days in the chief's village, incipient tensions between the Herskovitses and their servants were quietly smoothed over by Wolff, an effective mediator and "obviously very friendly with [the chief]." But after Wolff left on July 30, things quickly got out of hand. Jacoba, who in 1928 had worked so well with FSH and even named her baby after Herskovits, became surly and uncooperative, and Schloss, chosen by MJH as a guide because he had impressed him so favorably in 1928, became incensed at an accusation of two-timing the Herskovitses and turned against them, becoming (for reasons having nothing to do with field ethnography or Saramaka secrets) the direct instigator of their expulsion from the chief's village.

The blow-up that brought on the end occurred shortly before Wolff's departure, and simmered under the surface until a few days later.

We had a very unpleasant incident with Schloss,— Wolff advised us to get his note-book, and after a violent discussion he gave it to us. Apparently Lawton [the U.S. consul] & Stefan asked him to note down the resources of the river for them, and he promised. The nerve!—It is agreed that the book is to go to Mr. Van Haaren [the colonial secretary/attorney general], and if he decides Schloss is to have the book, he gets it.

The next day, Fann is still "getting on well with the women," collecting data on widowhood and religion, but "feels that the old fellow, for political reasons, is keeping things from getting to us." She passes her concerns on to Wolff, who "talked to the old man" and MJH held on to his guarded optimism. "Wolff has been marvellous.... We're here for 9 or 10 days on our own, and we hope for the best." Indeed, the next day (July 31) is "a better day; an excellent one, in fact." But on August 1 the diary begins with a "Grrr!"

> When we found Jacoba had been taking salt-meat when she said she didn't eat it and that tobacco supplies were low, we both blew up. Fann handled Jacoba without kid gloves for once, and as a result we ate cold food for supper, and J. has worked herself into an hysterical fever.

August 2 is recorded as "a worse day":

> I was about to test the [wax-cylinder] reproducer when Schloss came to me; the big fellow [chief] had wanted to know how much he was paid; how much Jacoba was paid; said we were rich and should pay him for the use of his house; what others had given him, and more along that line. Whether we're to be mulcted, or whether he talked to S[chloss] in order to induce us to go, we don't know. But we're alone in the interior.... What will happen no one can say, but we held a council of war and decided to act fast. We called the old chap in...and told him...we'd like to leave.

It seems clear what must have happened. On the heels of tensions that had been building for some time between the Herskovitses and their hired help, MJH accused Schloss of cheating by taking on a second job behind his back. Schloss, furious, complained to all within earshot, and eventually went directly to the chief, giving him an earful. Meanwhile, Jacoba, who had gripes of her own, took Schloss' side and spread her own stories to the Saramaka women doing laundry and dishwashing with her at the river's edge. Within the week, the chief had heard enough—from Schloss, from Jacoba, from the villagers—to conclude that the Herskovitses were trouble and, in the diplomatic fashion that befitted his office, he arranged to have them decide to leave.

The Birth of a Discipline?

> "From the family plots of the Jamaican hinterland,
> the Afro-religions of Brazil and Cuba, or the jazz
> music of Louisiana to the vitality of Haitian
> painting and music and the historical awareness of
> Suriname's maroons, the cultural practices that
> typify various African American populations appear
> to us as the product of a repeated miracle.... Their
> very existence is a continuing puzzle. For they were
> born against all odds."
>
> (Michel-Rolph Trouillot, 2002)

This is the Herskovitsian legacy at its finest, the
wonder we still sense at what Trouillot calls "the
miracle of creolization."

It would be foolish to maintain that Afro-
American Anthropology, or Afro-American Studies,
was born as the result of a near-immaculate conception in the Suriname bush. U.S. pioneers such as
W. E. B. Du Bois and Carter G. Woodson, Cubans
such as Fernando Ortiz, and Haitians such as Jean
Price-Mars—all of whom Herskovits corresponded
with and whose work he knew—had been carving out
chunks in this area of investigation for some time (as
had Brazilian scholars whose work MJH came to know
only later). Closer to home, scholars as diverse as Elsie
Clews Parsons (who not only was the Herskovitses'
patron for the Suriname project but had herself
conducted serious research on the African origins of
Bahamian and West Indian folktales), Zora Neale
Hurston (who had been MJH's research assistant for

his Harlem work in 1926), and Franz Boas, who was ultimately the granddady of the whole enterprise, certainly helped shape his developing consciousness, which was spelled out to some degree in his unsuccessful 1926 grant application. However, Herskovits specifically credited his intellectual turnabout—from emphasizing "The Negro's Americanism" (his chapter in Alain Locke's *The New Negro*) to proclaiming his bold comparative Afro-Americanist program—"essentially [to] findings of field research among the coastal and Bush Negroes of Dutch Guiana."

In part because of his sheer ambition and in part because of the workings of U.S. racism in the academy, the task of defining the field of Afro-American studies and training the first generation of academic specialists fell on the shoulders of MJH. His first clear formulation—"The New World Negro: The Statement of a Problem," in which he outlined the whole scientific programme for the *comparative* study of Africans in the diaspora (from the Suriname bush to the streets of Harlem)—was published in the *American Anthropologist* in early 1930, only months after the couple's return from Suriname.

Any assessment of the value of what emerged from those two summers' bubbling cauldron of professional ambitions and anxieties, ideas about a woman's place, Boasian models for data collecting, and colonial notions of comportment in the tropics depends heavily on subject position. Some younger, "postcolonial" scholars are now questioning the object that became known as Afro-American Anthropology, seeing it as based on the meretricious assumption that peoples of

African descent in the New World require a "science of culture" to provide them with the foundational guarantee of an authentic past. At the same time, many historians and anthropologists continue to engage questions that emerged directly out of the Herskovitsian programme, producing some of the most significant works of the past few years—in American History, for example, Ira Berlin's *Many Thousands Gone* and Philip D. Morgan's *Slave Counterpoint*. Such neo-Herskovitsian questions include: How "ethnically" homogeneous (or heterogeneous) were the enslaved Africans arriving in particular New World localities and what were the cultural consequences? By what processes did these Africans become African *Americans*? How quickly and in what ways did they and their African American offspring begin thinking and acting as members of new communities—that is, how rapid was creolization? In what ways did the African arrivants choose—and were they able—to continue particular ways of thinking and of doing things that came from the Old World? How did the various demographic profiles and social conditions of particular New World plantation settings encourage or inhibit these processes?

Scholars' answers to such questions are often at odds and the polemics can come close to fisticuffs. But whether they take their stand as self-described "Africa-centrists" (those, like Paul Lovejoy, John Thornton, or Michael Gomez, who argue that particular African ethnicities continued to play a major role in the Americas for many generations) or as what these latter like to call "creation theorists" (those, like

Sidney Mintz or ourselves, who argue for a scenario of more rapid creolization), all are in a real sense working within the *problématique* announced by MJH soon after his precipitous departure from the Saramaka chief's village. When the Herskovitses emerged from the "deep interior," they bore the seeds of a garden that many of us are still harvesting. And it remains as politically and ideologically charged today as when the Herskovitses first laid it out.

Although one current political reading of the Herskovitses' fieldwork would label them handmaidens of Dutch colonialism, this strikes us as both banal and a cheap shot. The character of their entourage, the style of their clothing and travel, and the nature of their interactions with Saramakas certainly supported colonial ideas of "racial" order. But this seems to have gone with the territory for most anthropologists who were out at the edge of someone's empire during the period. Some forty years later, when we arrived in Suriname, colonial officialdom had budged little. The district commissioner instructed us about proper comportment in the bush, and we went so far as to buy high-top anti-snake boots and special-issue army hammocks with zippered-in mosquito netting. But it being the 1960s rather than the 1920s, we threw away the boots as soon as we got upriver and never used the coffin-like hammocks, instead going barefoot throughout our stay and sleeping, like Saramaka couples, in a conjugal made-in-Brazil hammock. In the 1960s, it was not difficult to see continuing colonial practices as anachronistic; in the 1920s, they remained very much the order of the day.

But it is *not* anachronistic to characterize the Herskovitses' fieldwork as rushed and shoddy. While it may have been common for Boas' students, like Margaret Mead, to use their fieldwork mainly to demonstrate an argument they started out with, other young anthropologists of the day were working in native languages, overhearing and noting down conversations, and making careful observations of the minutiae of daily life. In other words, they were doing all the things Herskovits claimed an anthropologist should do but which we now know he did not do. Take, to mention just one example, Raymond Firth, who arrived on the Polynesian island of Tikopia in the same year that Herskovits first visited Saramaka and whose field work seems to have been everything the Herskovitses' was not.

The Herskovitses' Saramaka fieldwork also set a pattern that they were to follow in their influential research in Africa. Suzanne Blier's analysis of their fieldwork in Dahomey concludes that MJH was "a man in a hurry" whose interests were "more with ideas and large historical and social issues than with extensive and detailed field research." She calls attention to the brevity of their visit, the small number of informants interviewed (combined with claims, in their publications, that there were many more), the highly educated status of MJH's main informant, Prince René Aho, and the way he dominated the providing of information, the lack of systematic cross-checking of materials with different informants, the "relatively small number of ceremonies or rituals" actually observed, the "remarkable...sketchiness and brevity" of their fieldnotes compared to the substantial amounts of published material, and the importance of FSH's contributions to the ethnography. (Fortunately for African Studies, in which MJH held the first chair established in the U.S.A., as well as for Afro-American Studies, the vision of field research that they passed on to the next generation reflected their ideals more than their practices; many of their students conducted field research of a very different sort.)

The Herskovitses' Saramaka fieldwork and our own initial stays almost exactly bracket what George Stocking calls "the classic period of Anthropology" (the mid-1920s to the mid-1960s). What were the similarities and differences between methods, assumptions, and goals at the beginning and end of this era (above and beyond such things as pith helmets or women's delicate constitutions)? The Herskovitses' fieldwork *ideals* sound much like those we were taught to have four decades later: long-term residence in villages without mediators (servants, Western-educated natives), working in the native language, doing participant observation, and writing down a maximum of "data" to produce, some day, a near-encyclopedic ethnographic monograph. We shared the sheer excitement of experiencing "difference," some of the romantic primitivism, and a lot of the cultural relativism of the Herskovitses.

But our idea and theirs of what an ethnographic "fact" was differed significantly and lies at the root of more radical differences. Because their facts were largely unproblematized (the data were out there to be gathered in—steam-shovelled, as MJH put it—

and then simply written up), they didn't worry much about their sources or questions of representation once they could satisfy themselves that their informants weren't lying. When van Lier or Schmidt dictated accounts of the Saramaka political or kinship system to MJH they went straight into publications as the way it was. Normative behavior—the Saramakas do this or that and do not do thus and so—was the order of the day; culture was determinate and individual variation interesting only anecdotally.

By the early 1960s, however, we were at least beginning to be taught that culture (and social structure) was emergent, that it was both given *and* created on a daily basis through the interactions of individuals. This implied the central credo of our generation's fieldwork (or, at least, our version of it)—that the problems should emerge largely from the concerns of the people being studied, that in order to write an ethnography of Saramaka, one should start from what Saramakas themselves talked about (or chose not to talk about) among themselves, what they cared about, what they felt was important. It also implied an interest in what non-Saramakas said about Saramakas—but largely as a way of understanding stereotypes. And it explored Saramaka society and Saramaka individuals in relation to the wider world— that is, it covered areas of political and economic relations that were willfully erased in the Herskovitses' work. During the 1960s, both epistemological and ethical concerns in anthropology (and the other human sciences) unavoidably came to the fore. And though it is clear, with hindsight, that there were

regnant politics and poetics in "writing culture" at
both moments, it was only during the second that they
became clearly visible (and objects of reflection). One
might then situate our own early work in Saramaka as
having one foot in the deep interior and another
searching for solid ground in a paradigm (even today)
still under construction.

The career of Ruth Landes, who followed
Herskovits by a few years as a Boas student at
Columbia, sheds additional light on the birth of Afro-
American anthropology and on the ways gender, race,
fieldwork methodology, and professional ambition,
rivalry, and gatekeeping shaped the field. Landes, an
independent-minded woman with two American
Indian books already to her name who wished to
study the great black city of Salvador (Bahia, Brazil),
was first sent off for a preparatory year at Fisk
University (in Nashville) so that she could, among
other things, "get used to Negroes." But she got a
little closer than her mentor intended and had to be
hurried out before an interracial scandal became
public. And after the Bahia fieldwork for her book,
The City of Women, again showed too much familiarity—she became the frequent and fairly public
companion of the dapper Afro-Brazilian folklorist and
journalist Edison Carneiro—Herskovits (now a full
professor) black-balled her, warning her potential
employers about her "unorthodox" and "unscientific"
field methods. Her reward for a book that preco-
ciously theorized (or, at the least, foregrounded) race,
gender, and sexuality—but largely ignored
Herskovits' agenda of seeking African connections—

was to be barred, throughout a long career, from receiving any permanent job in the United States.

The Herskovitses' genealogical orientation, their search for African origins, was part and parcel of the Boasian legacy. (MJH had written in 1925, "any given culture is comprised of two elements, a certain amount, probably the smaller, which has originated within the group, and a much larger amount which has been borrowed.") Part of the anthropologist's modus operandi, then, was to trace traits present in one culture back to an ancestral one. At its extreme, this led MJH to draw a map that showed the purported West African origins of several Saramaka villages and clans—the village of "Kisi Ama" was traced to French Sudan, the Abaisa clan to Ivory Coast—but this kind of trait chasing, here based purely on similarities of names, was never systematically pursued by him. Nonetheless, the idea stuck, and before leaving for Africa in 1931 he wrote his old Suriname friend Wolff, referring to two of their servants/informants from 1929, that "We hope to be most of the time in Dahomey where Magdalena and Freddie's people come from."

The Herskovitsian genealogical imperative with its search for African roots gained a second life soon after MJH's death in 1963, but from largely independent sources. In the wake of the Civil Rights movement, ideas that valorized Blackness and Africanity—which had long been an undercurrent in U.S. identity politics (Du Bois, Garveyism, the New Negro Movement of the Harlem Renaissance)—blossomed as never before. From Alex Haley's *Roots* and

Robert Farris Thompson's *Flash of the Spirit* to the
African-names-for your-new-baby and 100-traditional-
African-hairstyles booklets at supermarket checkout
racks, from Harvard to the streets of Watts, Black was
Beautiful and roots were in. There is no doubt that
the staying power, within the academy and out, of
Herskovits' diasporic vision, and its revitalization
during the past several decades, has as much to do
with ongoing identity politics as with its originality or
truth. But hasn't that always been the case, certainly in
such ideologically charged fields as African American
(or other ethnic or feminist) studies?

Out of the anxieties, misperceptions, and
other fumblings and bumblings of the Herskovitses'
Saramaka fieldwork emerged a vision that has played
a signal role in African American studies ever since.
W. E. B. Du Bois, assessing Herskovits' *Myth of the
Negro Past*, argued that "no one hereafter writing on
the cultural accomplishments of the American Negro
can afford to be ignorant of its content and conclu-
sions" and Sidney W. Mintz wrote: "It is difficult to
imagine any serious consideration of the culture and
lives of Afro-Americans in the modern world which
could ignore what Herskovits explained to us half a
century ago."

Does this suggest that ethnographic details
don't matter? That the mere experience of being there
(even when understanding little "from the native's
point of view") can be sufficient for the development
of theoretical advances? Herskovits' "discovery" of
"Africa" in the Suriname bush, combined with a more
diluted version in the colony's capital, and then those

games of *wari* he played with men on the docks at British Caribbean ports on the way home, do seem to have sparked his pioneering programme, despite his misunderstandings in the field. That he never quite got the Saramaka ethnography right seems in the end not to have mattered much, to him or to anyone else. Go figure.

On the African Fringe

"Fandya continued to urge our staying. 'Ame'ika Fandya,' he said—the year before he had given his own name to the white man—'remain with us tonight and tomorrow.'"

According to MJH's diary, the name-giving occurred on 3 August 1928. Arriving in the village of Baikutu, MJH and Rogalli were taken to the house of the captain. "As we were introduced, I said thru Rogalli I didn't have a Djuka name, and I should have one. So he gave me his own—Frá-dya, right there—a very pretty gesture I thought." (In Saramaccan, *faándya* is the word for "fringe.") It is hardly surprising that when MJH returned the following year, the captain referred to him playfully as "American Fandya," in contradistinction to himself.

Coming upon this diary entry, we suddenly remembered a Saramaka woman from the chief's village who had once interrupted an interview about the aesthetics of patchwork textiles to reminisce about "some other Americans who came here a long time ago, in the time of Gaama Djankuso." Digging back into Sally's yellowing fieldnotes, we eventually located the interview in question, dated 8/4/76. Then in her sixties, Akundumini still had vivid memories of singing into the visitors' horn. "I wore only a small [adolescent] apron then," she said, "but I was already a very good singer!" She added, "The man's name was Afiika Faandya, and the person with him was called Faansisi—we all had big discussions about whether it was a man or a woman. Some people insisted it was his wife, but others didn't believe it, because of the pants."

Later, Sally noticed the discrepancy between *Rebel Destiny*, where Captain Fandya called MJH *Ame'ika Fandya*, and Akundu's version of the name, *Afiika Faandya*. On a subsequent field trip, she asked about it again, to see whether she had perhaps misheard. Akundu repeated that the man she had sung for was known to Saramakas from her village (the same village where MJH had so insistently prodded people about connections to their ancestral homeland) as *Afiika* ("African," not "American") *Faandya*— "African Fringe."

And then she and her elderly mother, Mbié, who had been invited to join the conversation, volunteered two other precious memories, making it clear that even if the Herskovitses had erased their servants from the narrative, the Saramakas had not. The notes record that these are the only other memory traces that the Herskovitses' stay in the chief's village, a half-century earlier, had left: "Those people," Akundu reminisced, "had a woman who cooked for them named Koba." And then Mbié added flatly: "Their Creole man from the city made trouble with them and Gaama Djankuso told them they had to leave." ■

Recommended Readings

The full list of references cited in the text can be found on the web at: www.prickly-paradigm.com/catalog.html

Blier, Suzanne Preston. 1989. "Field Days: Melville J. Herskovits in Dahomey." *History in Africa* 16:1-22.

Cole, Sally. 1995. "Ruth Landes and the Early Ethnography of Race and Gender." In Ruth Behar and Deborah A. Gordon (eds.), *Women Writing Culture*. Berkeley, University of California Press, pp. 166-185.

Herskovits, Frances S. (ed.). 1966. *The New World Negro [collected essays by Melville J. Herskovits]*. Bloomington, Indiana University Press.

Herskovits, Melville J. 1925. "The Negro's Americanism." In Alain Locke (ed.), *The New Negro*. New York, Charles and Albert Boni, pp. 353-360.

Herskovits, Melville J. 1941. *The Myth of the Negro Past*. New York: Harper & Brothers.

Herskovits, Melville J. & Frances S. Herskovits. 1934. *Rebel Destiny: Among the Bush Negroes of Dutch Guiana*. New York: McGraw-Hill.

Herskovits, Melville J. & Frances S. Herskovits. 1936. *Suriname Folk-lore. Columbia University Publications in Anthropology* 27. New York: Columbia University Press.

Jackson, Walter. 1986. "Melville Herskovits and the Search for Afro-American Culture." In George W. Stocking, Jr. (ed.), *Malinowski, Rivers, Benedict and Others: Essays on Culture and Personality, History of Anthropology 4*. Madison, University of Wisconsin Press, pp. 95-126.

Kahn, Morton C. 1931. *Djuka: The Bush Negroes of Dutch Guiana.* New York: Viking.

Maurer, Bill. 2002. "Fact and Fetish in Creolization Studies: Herskovits and the Problem of Induction, or, Guinea Coast, 1593." *New West Indian Guide* 76:5-22.

Mintz, Sidney W. 1964. "Melville J. Herskovits and Caribbean Studies: A Retrospective Tribute." *Caribbean Studies* 4(2):42-51.

Mintz, Sidney W. & Richard Price. 1992. *The Birth of African-American Culture.* Boston: Beacon Press.

Price, Richard. 2001. "The Miracle of Creolization: A Retrospective." *New West Indian Guide* 75:35-64.

Price, Sally & Richard Price. 1999. *Maroon Arts: Cultural Vitality in the African Diaspora.* Boston: Beacon Press.

Scott, David. 1991. "That Event, This Memory: Notes on the Anthropology of African Diasporas in the New World." *Diaspora* 1(3):261-284.

Simpson, George Eaton. 1973. *Melville J. Herskovits.* New York: Columbia University Press.

Trouillot, Michel-Rolph. 2002. "Culture on the Edges: Caribbean Creolization in Historical Context." In Brian Keith Axel (ed.), *From the Margins: Historical Anthropology and its Futures.* Durham, NC, Duke University Press, pp. 189-210.

Vandercook, John Womack. 1926. *"Tom-Tom."* New York: Harper & Brothers.

Yelvington, Kevin A. (ed.). 2004. *Afro-Atlantic Dialogues: Anthropology in the Diaspora.* Santa Fe, NM: School of American Research.

Look for these titles by Prickly Paradigm, and others to come:

Paradigm 1
Marshall Sahlins
Waiting for Foucault, Still

Paradigm 2
Bruno Latour
War of the Worlds:
What about Peace?

Paradigm 3
Richard Rorty, Derek Nystrom, and Kent Puckett
Against Bosses, Against Oligarchies:
A Conversation with Richard Rorty

Paradigm 4
Deirdre McCloskey
The Secret Sins of Economics

Paradigm 5
Thomas Frank
New Consensus for Old:
Cultural Studies from Left to Right

Paradigm 6
Michael Silverstein
Talking Politics:
The Substance of Style from Abe to "W"

Paradigm 7
Chris Lehmann
Revolt of the Masscult

Paradigm 8
Donna Haraway
The Companion Species Manifesto:
Dogs, People, and Significant Otherness

Paradigm 9
Eliot Weinberger
9/12:
New York After

Paradigm 10
James Clifford
On the Edges of Anthropology (Interviews)

Paradigm 11
Magnus Fiskesjö
The Thanksgiving Turkey Pardon, the Death of Teddy's Bear,
and the Sovereign Exception of Guantánamo

Paradigm 12
Richard Price and Sally Price
The Root of Roots:
Or, How Afro-American Anthropology Got its Start

Paradigm 13
James Elkins
What Happened to Art Criticism?